PRAISE FOR *CREATU*

"The topic is relevant. The author is reliable. The material is Bible based. A perfect recipe resulting in a great read. The topic? Habits. Those patterns of behavior that direct our days. The author? Steve Poe. One of America's great pastors, dearly loved by his church and highly regarded by colleagues (like myself) worldwide. The material? God's Word. And God has a word for you and your habits. This book will help you create life-giving ones."

—MAX LUCADO, *NEW YORK TIMES* BESTSELLING AUTHOR

"There's no shortcut to any place that's worth going. Steve helps us own and tackle the deeper heart issues that fuel our bad habits so we can experience all that God intends for our lives."

—DAVE RAMSEY, *NEW YORK TIMES* BESTSELLING AUTHOR OF *THE TOTAL MONEY MAKEOVER* AND RADIO HOST

"Any change, even an incremental one, can make a huge difference over the course of your life. It's never too late to let God help you change the trajectory of your life. Steve Poe will help you see just that."

—KYLE IDLEMAN, SENIOR PASTOR OF SOUTHEAST CHRISTIAN CHURCH AND AUTHOR OF *NOT A FAN* AND *DON'T GIVE UP*

"Some preach with conviction; some live with conviction—Steve does both. His desire to help people find the grace of God and live with that grace, break their old habits, and become the people God intends, can be seen through the pages of this book. I love his line, 'most of us are like the rest of us.' Steve paints a picture of who we are and who we can be in Jesus—don't miss reading *Creatures of Habit*."

—RICK RUSAW, FORMER LEAD PASTOR OF LIFEBRIDGE CHRISTIAN CHURCH, AUTHOR, AND CEO OF SPIRE NETWORK

"All of us have a few pesky habits that always seem to hold us back. Old habits never change until we have a new approach to conquering them. This book is your guide to do just that!"

—ASHLEY WOOLRIDGE, SENIOR PASTOR OF CHRIST'S CHURCH OF THE VALLEY

"Pastor Poe's book provides simple, understandable explanations and application of complex biblical standards. He encourages and motivates his readers to engage in self-evaluation and communal confession in order to conquer pernicious habits and launch life-giving habits. Your life and your family will benefit from [you] reading *Creatures of Habit*."

—ALICE BENTON, PSYD, CLINICAL PSYCHOLOGIST

"*Creatures of Habit* unlocks the habit power that God has already built into you, turning your innate wiring into a spiritual strength that leads to a better life. Steve Poe has given us a real gift in this book, the best Christian book on habit formation I've ever read. If you want more freedom, success, joy, and spiritual impact in your life, I highly recommend *Creatures of Habit*."

—JOHN S. DICKERSON, LEAD PASTOR OF CONNECTION POINTE CHRISTIAN CHURCH, NATIONALLY AWARDED JOURNALIST, AND BESTSELLING AUTHOR OF *JESUS SKEPTIC*

"I have to be careful endorsing this book because my friend Steve called out flattery and exaggeration as part of the bad habits *some people* might have. So, I'll just be honest. Thankfully he didn't call me out in any of the chapters, but I was amazed at how much I saw myself in so many of them. I believe the reason most of us don't grow deeper in our lives is just a blatant *lack* of honesty, and this book will help you so much. Don't skim through it. Not only will it help you identify issues, this book is *so practical*. I also would like to say that you are reading a book written by one of the most godly men I know. I'm not saying he's an expert at all this, but I am saying that if there one person I'd like to read on the subject, Steve is the guy."

—TIM HARLOW, SENIOR PASTOR OF PARKVIEW CHRISTIAN CHURCH AND AUTHOR OF *WHAT MADE JESUS MAD?*

"*Creatures of Habit* is a gateway to personal and spiritual breakthrough. The wisdom in this book is second to none and will help any person who is stuck and overwhelmed by life's greatest temptations."

—STEVE CARTER, PASTOR AND AUTHOR OF *THE THING BENEATH THE THING*

"*Creatures of Habit* is a timely book for today's world. Steve Poe invites you to authentically examine the harmful, unseen places in your heart and life. More importantly, he equips you with practical steps that lead to change. This book will help you begin the process of letting go of what hinders you and fully seize all God has called you to be and do."

—ROB HOSKINS, PRESIDENT OF ONEHOPE AND COAUTHOR OF *CHANGE YOUR WORLD*

"When I first glanced at the table of contents, I never dreamed that *every* single chapter would convict, challenge, and inspire me—and yet, each one did. Healthy habits are life-giving, and bad habits become increasingly destructive. So, don't read this book unless you are willing to look inward and get to the root of your problems. But if you do put into practice Steve's suggestions, I promise it will positively transform the trajectory of your life."

—DAVE STONE, FORMER SENIOR PASTOR OF SOUTHEAST CHRISTIAN CHURCH

"It is always a series of small habits [formed] over a long period of time that transforms a good athlete into a great one or makes an ordinary leader into an outstanding one. If you want more of God's best in your life, *Creatures of Habit* gives you a handbook for discovering the spiritual power of consistent incremental change in your life. I highly recommend it!"

—DAVE FERGUSON, LEAD PASTOR OF COMMUNITY CHRISTIAN CHURCH AND COAUTHOR OF *BLESS*

"No matter how good a book, I can't recommend it unless I can personally recommend the author. Because Steve Poe is the real deal, I jumped at the chance to recommend his book *Creatures of Habit*. It's an important, valuable, and relevant book. Though habits play a significant role in our spiritual lives, most people miss it. Steve doesn't. He sees and addresses it clearly. . . . Steve will help you to understand what it takes and then guide you through the difficult journey of applying it in your daily life. My prayer is that you'll accept and embrace his help."

—BRAD POWELL, LEAD PASTOR OF NORTHRIDGE CHURCH AND AUTHOR OF *CHANGE YOUR CHURCH FOR GOOD*

"Let's be honest: our habits will either make us or break us. I once heard that a good golf coach can identify the ten things wrong with your swing; a great golf coach can identify the one that is causing the other nine. My good friend Steve Poe is a great coach. Chapter by chapter he helps us to see the one thing that we need to focus on that can set us up to win at life and he provides simple, accessible steps to get there. I picked my 'one' chapter to focus on. I invite you to do the same."

—RANDY FRAZEE, LEAD TEACHING PASTOR OF WESTSIDE CHURCH AND AUTHOR OF *HIS MIGHTY STRENGTH*

"This book will make you uncomfortable in all the best ways. Steve Poe has a special gift of peeling back the layers that often prevent us from seeing our souls accurately and shows us how to access the power to be the people deep down we all want to be consistently."

—GENE APPEL, SENIOR PASTOR OF EASTSIDE CHRISTIAN CHURCH

"Bad habits can be like magnets that pull you away from God's best. In *Creatures of Habit*, Steve gives you some practical steps to break these habits in your life."

—BRIAN TOME, SENIOR PASTOR OF CROSSROADS CHURCH AND AUTHOR OF *MOVE, THE MAN DEVOTIONAL*

"We all know about vices. Sure, I *struggle* with . . . you name it. But in *Creatures of Habit* Steve offers a paradigm most of us haven't considered: What if that thing is more insidious than a 'little struggle' but something that is really driving me more than I care to admit? And once I recognize it, what do I do about it? Steve has broken down overcoming dangerous habits into actionable steps. I'm grateful for Steve's voice that's leading so many people toward fruitful, free living."

—DAVE DUMMITT, SENIOR PASTOR OF WILLOW CREEK COMMUNITY CHURCH

"Has your world felt uncertain in the last year or so? Whose hasn't? If you're like me, you're probably looking for ways to form habits that can bring normalcy and positive direction to your life. Pastor Steve Poe has given the world a gift in *Creatures of Habit*. It's not just a book to give you discipline but is a book about forming habits that are grounded in a Jesus-centered life. Find a copy. Read it today. And you will find direction and blessing."

—WILLIAM VANDERBLOEMEN, FOUNDER AND CEO OF VANDERBLOEMEN SEARCH GROUP

CREATURES OF HABIT

CREATURES OF HABIT

Breaking the Habits Holding You Back from God's Best

STEVE POE

An Imprint of Thomas Nelson

Published in Nashville, Tennessee, by Nelson Books, an imprint of Thomas Nelson. Nelson Books and Thomas Nelson are registered trademarks of HarperCollins Christian Publishing, Inc.

Published in association with the literary agency of WordServe Literary Group, Ltd., www.wordserveliterary.com.

Thomas Nelson titles may be purchased in bulk for educational, business, fundraising, or sales promotional use. For information, please e-mail SpecialMarkets@ThomasNelson.com.

ISBN 978-1-4002-2342-8 (TP)
ISBN 978-1-4002-2343-5 (eBook)

Library of Congress Cataloging-in-Publication Data

Names: Poe, Steve, 1957- author.
Title: Creatures of habit : breaking the habits holding you back from God's best / Steve Poe.
Description: Nashville, Tennessee : Nelson Books, [2021] | Includes bibliographical references. | Summary: "Beloved pastor Steve Poe helps Christians identify and break free from the destructive patterns that are keeping them from the joy-filled, flourishing life Jesus promised"-- Provided by publisher.
Identifiers: LCCN 2020047252 (print) | LCCN 2020047253 (ebook) | ISBN 9781400223428 | ISBN 9781400223435 (ebook)
Subjects: LCSH: Habit breaking--Religious aspects--Christianity.
Classification: LCC BV4598.7 .P64 2021 (print) | LCC BV4598.7 (ebook) | DDC 248.4--dc23
LC record available at https://lccn.loc.gov/2020047252
LC ebook record available at https://lccn.loc.gov/2020047253

Printed in the United States of America

21 22 23 24 25 LSC 10 9 8 7 6 5 4 3 2 1

To my wife, Sandy, who is still the most beautiful woman I know.

You are my best friend and soul mate. From the first time we met, you stole my heart. I just had no idea life with you would be this special. I would have never completed this book without your continual words of encouragement.

CONTENTS

FOREWORD

by Stephen Arterburn

In the twelfth chapter of Mark, a teacher of religious law asked Jesus about the greatest of all the commandments. After Jesus answered, the teacher responded to what Jesus said by summing it up and affirming that loving God and your neighbor is far greater than offering sacrifices. Jesus told him, "You are not far from the kingdom of God" (v. 34 NIV). What a sad reality for that teacher. He *almost* got it right. He was close, but not on point. It is not a small thing to *almost* be part of the kingdom of God.

There are a lot of faithful churchgoers who are not lost for eternity, but they are living in the "land of almost." They are *almost* loving to their spouses. They are *almost* godly parents. They are *almost* free of an addiction. They are *almost* a lot of things, but not quite. They are *almost* living a Christlike life with character and integrity. They are *almost* there, but still a long way from God's best for their lives. They try harder and harder to turn their lives around, but they get stuck because they focus on changing the visible symptoms rather than transforming the invisible defects that are the real problems in need of resolution and healing. What does it profit a person to change their eating habits for a while if they don't deal with the worry that leads them to eat compulsively? It is only a matter of time before the weight will be back on. It does not help if you try to stop using pornography but don't resolve the anger and resentment that fuels the demeaning and dehumanizing use.

So many of our problems have visible signs that show up on the surface. These problems have emotional and psychological symptoms, but they need a spiritual solution. Too often those who struggle fall into the trap of treating the visible signs or the emotional symptoms and not going deep enough to discover, understand, and heal the deeper wounds of dysfunction.

If you have suffered and struggled with things of the flesh or dark matters of the soul, then *Creatures of Habit* is the right book at the right time. Steve Poe goes deep below the obvious problems to address the deeper issues driving the different and deficient ways we act out. If you are working too much, just changing your schedule does nothing to heal the inferiority and fear that drive you to ignore those who love you, including God. This book will lead you to look at the pride and worry of a workaholic and provide a path to eradicate these two sources of inner decay. If you simply commit to stop looking at pornography, sadly, unresolved anger will drive you back to it. Going deeper to resolve and heal the anger elevates you to the life of integrity God has had waiting for you since he thought you up. A life lived to the full.

I think the chapter on cynicism is worth the entire price of the book. Cynics are often the ringleaders in the land of almost. This chapter reveals a way to rip out the roots of cynicism and to live with genuine hope and godly optimism. No longer will people avoid you or ignore you because they don't want your negativity to infect their souls. In the chapter on lying, you will see that none of the other problems can be treated, healed, or resolved unless you are committed to radical honesty. This is the big one, and you will find big relief if you struggle just to tell the truth. While liars are at home in the land of almost, honest truth-tellers move toward authentic sharing in the "land of all-in."

This is not *almost* a great book. It is a deep and practical guide to dredge out the depths of your character and reach the heights of godly living in the will of God. This is how you get out of being *almost* committed and *almost* Christlike and *almost* godly. It is an invitation to being all in. To that end, I want to suggest that you read this book slowly. Consider the questions that are asked at the end of the book for each chapter. Write down your responses. Implement the advice Steve gives, and in a few months, you might be surprised at how different your answers are. If there was ever a book to actually go deeper when it invites you to go deeper, this is the one. The whole book is about changing the deeper areas that are too often neglected.

I am honored to have the title of teaching pastor of Northview Church, which is one of the twenty largest churches in America. Last year it was the third fastest-growing US church. This is where Steve Poe replaced the founding pastor fifteen years ago and still serves as lead pastor. Steve *leads*! I have watched him with his incredible wife, Sandy, and listened to him teach some of the best messages I have heard. I always listen with a bit of a critical ear, and he is spot-on in every message. I have served in a very small way in comparison to his stellar team, whose standard is connected, quality, and redemptive ministry. Steve is a true and genuine man of integrity, character, and compassion, and his great team members are the same. They do so well in meeting the needs of those they serve. They all care deeply about those who attend, which is a reflection of Steve's heart. Four of our campuses are in Indiana state prisons. You don't open churches in prisons to increase tithes and offerings; you do it because that is what Christ told you to do. What I'm saying is that what you read in *Creatures of Habit* comes from the heart of a man who has a habit of meeting needs through ministry.

Having said all that, I want to assure you that although I might be a bit biased, that is not why I love this book. I love it because I love to see people transform their lives, and I believe *Creatures of Habit* is going to help thousands of people do just that.

Stephen Arterburn is the teaching pastor of Northview Church. He is the founder of New Life Ministries and host of the *New Life Live* radio program. He is also the creator of the Women of Faith conferences attended by more than five million women, with more than five hundred thousand making first-time decisions for Christ. He is the bestselling author of books such as *Every Man's Battle* and has more than twelve million books in print. He is also the editor of fifteen study Bibles, including *Every Man's Bible*, the bestselling men's study Bible, as well as the *Spiritual Renewal Bible*, which won Bible of the Year, and *The Life Recovery Bible*, which has sold more than three million copies. He can be reached at Steve.Arterburn@NorthviewChurch.us or 1-800-NEW-LIFE.

CHANGING OUR OLD WAYS

We are what we repeatedly do. Excellence, then, is not an act, but a habit.

—Will Durant

I once heard a story about a young girl who was driving over a bridge in East Los Angeles when she fell asleep. She hit the guardrail, and her car flipped and was left dangling over the pavement far below by its left rear wheel. The only thing holding the girl in her vehicle was the seat belt. One false move could have spelled disaster. For the next two and a half hours, rescuers desperately worked to pull this girl to safety. One of the firemen later commented that the entire time they were trying to rescue her, she kept yelling at them over and over: "I'll do it myself! I'll do it myself!"

I'm not sure if she had hit her head or was confused—whatever the case, it was irrational to think she could get out of such a predicament on her own. Yet I've noticed that many times, when it comes to our spiritual lives, we react the same way. Our sins or our bad habits plunge us into terrible circumstances, yet somehow we are convinced that if we just try a little harder or do more good deeds, everything will work out. And we, too, find ourselves saying, "I can do it myself! I don't need God's help—or anyone else's for that matter. I can handle this!"

I believe the turning point in many of our lives comes when we get past the delusion that we can fix our brokenness ourselves. The truth is, we need God's help! I love what Paul said: "Don't be so naive and self-confident. You're not exempt. You could fall flat on your face as easily as anyone else. Forget about *self-confidence*; it's useless. Cultivate *God-confidence*" (1 Cor. 10:12 THE MESSAGE, emphasis mine).

As we learn to put our faith and our trust in Christ, the Holy Spirit begins the process of making us more like him. Paul said, "So I say, let the Holy Spirit guide your lives. Then you won't be doing what your sinful nature craves" (Gal. 5:16).

In many ways our relationship with Christ is like a partnership. God is faithful to do his part. Through his Spirit he will lead us to do what is right. The question is whether we will follow. One of the best ways to follow the Spirit's lead is by adopting spiritual disciplines, which are nothing more than regular practices that eventually become spiritual habits that help us walk faithfully with the Lord.

We need the habits that engage our mind and heart with God. And few things can have a greater impact on us than improving the habits we create.

A habit is a behavior that has been repeated enough times that it has become second nature or automatic for us. And every day of our lives we are either reinforcing old habits or forming new ones. Often the word *habit* brings with it many negative connotations, including harmful behaviors like lying or repeatedly using drugs or alcohol (to the point of addiction). Or the habits could be smaller annoyances like biting your fingernails or smacking your lips. On the other hand, some habits can be positive—and may even save your life.

I was reminded of this when I was teaching my grandson to drive a car. He was doing a great job, but every time he needed to make a right turn, he would forget to first look left to make sure the coast was clear. He also kept forgetting to use his turn signal. (My wife says he learned that from me.) Working with him on his driving skills made me very much aware of how many things we do in life out of habit.

Positive or negative, habits are born out of the brilliance of our Creator. By making it possible for us to develop habits, God saved us from having to weigh the same decisions over and over again. They often become virtually automatic. The key is for Jesus to be reflected in those habits, which will happen if he is the most important thing in our lives. For instance, if we put Jesus first, then telling the truth can become a habit or starting our day with prayer can become second nature.

If you were to assess any person's habits, you would see what really captures his or her heart because our habits reveal what's important to us. Some might say I'm a pastor, a teacher, an attorney, or an electrician. Actually, those are occupations or professions; who I am is a follower of Christ, a child of God. As Scripture says, "God decided in advance to adopt us into his own family by bringing us to himself through Jesus Christ. This is what he wanted to do, and it gave him great pleasure" (Eph. 1:5). I belong to God and therefore my desire is to have Jesus reflected in my habits, showing that he is more important to me than anything else. So, every step I take toward forming godly habits is a personal vote for my identity in Christ.

The best way to form godly habits is to focus on who we want to become, not on what we want to achieve. Forming these habits is the path to demonstrating to the world that you are a child of God. (If you don't think people perceive you as a child of God, then it might just be that you need to change some of the habits in your life.) God created us to be action oriented. So in each chapter of this book, I share several steps you can take to break the bad habits that are keeping you from God's best and replace them with healthy spiritual habits.

But before you take any steps to break a habit, you have to first *own it*. It is very hard to break a habit if you are not even aware it's a problem. So with every chapter I will remind you of how important it is that we *own* the problem. For each topic I will encourage you to ask yourself questions such as:

- Has this become a habit in my life?
- Is it affecting my relationship with Christ?
- Is it affecting my relationship with others?
- Is it affecting my attitude in a negative way?
- Is it keeping me from becoming the person God wants me to become?

Honestly answering these simple questions can help you decide if this topic is a problem for you. If you decide that it is, then begin to work through the steps outlined in that chapter.

People want to believe that as a pastor I never have any problems. They want to believe that I have a perfect marriage, that my faith is never tested, and that I'm never tempted. Nothing could be further from the truth. All of us have areas in our lives that we struggle with—habits that we have allowed to divert our course from our identity in Christ. And if we ignore them long enough, they will collide with our faith—causing us to careen off the bridge of life. Like you, I have struggled with every topic in this book (and then some). Each chapter addresses a specific bad habit and then provides practical ideas on how to break it. At the end of the book you will find questions for further reflection if you want to go deeper or use it as a study guide for your small group. If you are a pastor and looking for a helpful sermon series for your church, you can find the manuscripts to my sermons on my website, www.StevePoeMinistries.com/Resources. If you are not a pastor, you might want to give your pastor a copy of this book.

A habit is like a double-edged sword. It can destroy you or build you up. If you ignore a bad habit it will become a stronghold in your life, and strongholds are extremely difficult to get rid of. So it's important that you identify the bad habits in your life and deal with them.

Jesus once passed by a blind man named Bartimaeus, who cried out to him. When Jesus heard him, he said, "What do you want me to do for you?" (Mark 10:46–52 NIV).

Don't you think Jesus knew this blind man wanted to be healed? Certainly! But Jesus wanted the blind man to first call it out, to identify the problem before he would heal him.

That's my hope for this book: that you will identify your bad habit and then take the necessary steps to break the habit keeping you from being all that God wants you to be.

I believe God is calling you to change, to have the audacity to say, "Enough is enough! I want people to clearly see that I am a child of God."

Let's get started!

1

PRIDE

There is an old urban legend about a navy warship sailing through fog one night when a distant light appeared directly ahead. As the light continued to get brighter, the captain came to the helm of the ship to assess the situation. About the same time a voice came over the radio and said, "The vessel traveling eighteen knots on a 220 heading, you need to adjust your course thirty degrees."

The captain got on the radio and responded, "This is the vessel on the 220 heading. You adjust *your* course thirty degrees!"

Then came the reply. "Negative, Captain. Adjust *your* course—now."

Irritated, the captain replied, "I am a captain in the US Navy. Whom am I speaking to?"

"I am an ensign in the US Coast Guard."

The captain said, "Then I suggest you adjust your course."

"No, sir. I suggest you adjust *yours* immediately."

"Son, we are a US Navy warship."

"Well, sir, we are a lighthouse. I think you should change course."

This is a picture of pride. We exhibit pride when we are so focused on our own perceived importance that we see ourselves as being bigger and more important than everyone else. The reality is that some things in life are bigger than you and me. Obviously God is one of them, and like a lighthouse, he is immovable.

When you think of pride, does it strike you as good or bad? Certainly pride can be looked at in different ways. Many view pride as a virtue. As a parent I'm proud of my two kids for the healthy and productive ways they live their lives. We like it when someone says, "I'm proud of you." We want our neighbors to display pride of ownership in the way they care for their homes. We appreciate people who take pride in the way they look or behave. All of these things communicate a positive kind of pride.

But pride isn't always positive. When the Bible speaks about the dangers of pride, it's speaking of the self-centered type. Paul writes in Romans 12:3, "Don't think you are better than you really are. Be honest in your evaluation of yourselves, measuring yourselves by the faith God has given us." Pride becomes sinful when it creates a feeling of superiority over others. It becomes sinful when you refuse to admit to any imperfections in your life. Self-centered pride is like an itch that constantly needs to be scratched. It's a need to always be the center of attention. Alice Roosevelt Longworth, one of President Theodore Roosevelt's daughters, said, "My father wants to be the corpse at every funeral, the bride at every wedding, and the baby at every christening."[1]

The Bible is hard on pride because pride keeps us from acknowledging the sin in our lives. Not only will self-centered pride keep you from God, it will damage other relationships in your life. I have seen marriages destroyed, families torn apart, friendships lost, all because a prideful person wouldn't acknowledge his mistakes, wouldn't admit when he was wrong, wouldn't apologize, and refused to compromise on petty issues. Pride keeps us from being totally honest with one another. We would rather have people admire the person we pretend to be than to love the person we really are.

C. S. Lewis called it "the Great Sin." He said:

> There is one vice of which no man in the world is free; which everyone in the world loathes when he sees it in someone else and of which hardly any people, except Christians, ever imagine that they are guilty themselves. . . . There is no fault which makes a man more unpopular, and no fault which we are more unconscious of in ourselves. And the more we have it ourselves, the more we dislike it in others. . . .
>
> According to Christian teachers, the essential vice, the utmost evil, is pride. Unchastity, anger, greed, drunkenness, and all that are mere fleabites in comparison. It was through pride that the Devil became the Devil: Pride leads to every other vice. It is the complete anti-God state of mind.[2]

The reason I chose to begin this book by talking about pride is because it's typically viewed as the most problematic habit a person can have. A self-centered person puts his own wants and desires before everything else. And all other bad habits or sinful acts are birthed out of that mindset. Take, for instance, the habit of lying. Why would a person lie? To influence things for her own benefit. Or what about adultery? Why would a person break his marriage vows? Because of his desire for self-gratification.

Most crimes committed today are birthed out of self-centeredness. People break the law to fulfill their own selfish desires. Whether it be cheating, fighting, abusing someone, stealing, committing rape, getting revenge, or even killing someone, in most cases those actions are born out of self-centeredness.

Pride in its worst form is commonly referred to as narcissism, which is marked by extreme selfishness or an overestimation of one's talents or importance. It's important to note that those with diagnosed narcissistic personality disorder will need professional help. Self-centered pride, on the other hand, is something all of us struggle with to one degree or another.

Do you remember when the comedian Jeff Foxworthy used to do the line, "You might be a redneck if . . ."? Well, you might be self-centered if . . . you know all the words to the song "My Way." You might be self-centered if . . . your favorite picture at home is the mirror. You might be self-centered if . . . you're on a date and say, "Enough talk about me . . . let's talk about what you think of me."

We laugh, but if I am self-centered, then my world revolves around the unholy trinity: Me, Myself, and I. It's what the Bible would call a problem of the flesh. The good news is that when you invite Christ into your life, that should all begin to change. Scripture says if anyone is in Christ, he or she is a new creation, the old is gone and the new has come (2 Cor. 5:17). Jesus wants to transform your life so you can exemplify Christ by the way you live. And of course, the nature of Christ was that he always put the needs of others before his own, and he commanded us to do the same. Paul talked about this: "Do nothing out of selfish ambition or vain conceit. Rather, in humility value others above yourselves, not looking to your own interests but each of you to the interests of the others" (Phil. 2:3–4 NIV).

Paul was trying to help his readers see that self-centered pride is at the very heart of the sinful nature. In fact, it was self-centered pride that led Eve to eat of the forbidden fruit back in Genesis 3. And to this day, thousands of years later, the struggle of the believer is still whether we are going to follow our own independent, selfish way or God's way. And when we refuse to do it God's way, we create this bad habit of self-centered pride, or a me-first mindset.

Pride is a mindset for a reason. It's what you set your mind on, what you think on. Consider the person who is struggling with jealousy. What do you think is dominating his thought process? Himself! He is looking at what someone else has and wishing he had it. If he truly regarded the other person as more important than himself, he would be happy for them rather than fretting over his own shortfall.

When I first went into pastoral ministry and was pastoring a very small church, it was hard not to be jealous of churches that were growing. I knew I should be happy for them, but I wanted it to be our church that grew.

Or how many husbands or wives have damaged the spirit of their spouse with their cutting remarks? There have been so many times I have said something hurtful to my wife. Do you think I was considering her when I spoke those words? No! I was thinking about my own perceived injustice or something that didn't go the way I thought it should have gone. We can all be guilty of hurting others when we allow pride to control us.

What about the man or woman viewing pornography? Do you think they really care about the person they are lusting after? Of course not! Again, the focus is on themselves. If a person is married and looking at porn, do you think they are considering the feelings of their spouse? No, they are thinking only about their own self-gratification.

Friends, the list could go on and on:

Bitterness says, "Look what they did to *me*!"
Unforgiveness says, "You have no idea how they have wronged *me*."
Greed says, "*I* must have more."
Gossip says, "*I* want all the dirty little details."

I would guess that self-centered pride affects your thoughts, decisions, values, and relationships more than you could ever imagine. Jesus knew that was the case with his disciples. After they had been under his teaching for a couple of years, they were still having a hard time understanding the importance of putting others first. You would think Jesus could have simply said, "Guys, this me-first mindset that you have is wrong, and it has got to go." But he didn't and the problem continued.

In Mark 8 Jesus told them he was going to lay down his life and suffer many things, and that he would be killed, and after three days he would rise again. Peter then pulled Jesus off to the side and rebuked him, saying, "You've got to stop talking like that!"

The problem was that Peter and the other disciples were dreaming of a day when Jesus would overthrow the Roman government and set up his Kingdom here on earth. The disciples imagined themselves in a place of great power and authority. So this idea that Jesus would suffer and be killed did not fit in the future they saw for themselves. And honestly, at this point I don't think Peter really cared about the lost condition of mankind; he was concerned only with his own position of influence.

So Jesus rebuked Peter and said, "Get behind me, Satan!" (How would you feel if Jesus called you the devil?) "You do not have in mind the concerns of God, but merely human concerns" (Mark 8:33 NIV). In other words, "Peter, you don't care about anybody but yourself!" That was a pretty strong rebuke from Jesus. I think he wanted Peter, as well as the rest of us, to understand that self-centered pride is birthed from the devil himself.

When you and I continue to live in self-centered pride, we are also promoting the devil's agenda. While Jesus wants you to put *him* on the throne of your life, the devil wants you to put *yourself* on the throne of your life. That might surprise you, but it's true. The devil is not trying to get you to be a devil worshiper. He knows that if he can get you to be self-centered, if he can get you to be self-focused, you will only further his agenda! He won't worry about you serving God because he knows, as long you are self-centered, you will ultimately move against the purposes and plans of God.

After Jesus rebuked Peter, he called everyone else over so he could help them see the problem. He said that whoever wanted to be his disciple must deny his self-centered pride and selfish ambition because he would never experience true satisfaction otherwise. But before we throw stones at the disciples, we should admit that we struggle in this area too.

In the very next chapter, Mark 9, we see that pride continued to be a problem. The disciples had argued, and Jesus asked them what they had been arguing about. "But they kept quiet because on the way they had argued about who was the greatest" (Mark 9:34 NIV). Are you kidding me? Jesus had just talked to them about this me-first mindset, and yet a few hours later they were arguing about who was going to be the greatest!

In Mark 10 it says, "Then James and John, the sons of Zebedee, came to him. 'Teacher,' they said, 'we want you to do for us whatever we ask'" (v. 35 NIV). Is that not the epitome of self-centeredness? And yet, doesn't it sound like a lot of Christians today? "Jesus, this is the person I want to marry. Work it out." "Jesus, this is the house we want to buy, so make our bid be the one." "Jesus, this is the job I want, so make sure I get it." And if that person doesn't want to marry us or we don't get the house or the job, we are upset with Jesus. Why? Because it's all about *our* selfish desires; there was no consideration of whether or not it was even part of God's plan for us.

For the third time Jesus tried to explain to them: "The Son of Man did not come to be served, but to serve, and to give his life as a ransom for many" (Mark 10:45 NIV). Jesus was saying, "Guys, I'm not asking you to do anything I haven't already modeled for you. I have tried to live my life so you can see what it really means to be a humble servant."

So then, how do we get rid of this pride? The real key to breaking any bad habit is to have a plan. Without a plan we will just gravitate back to whatever is comfortable.

The best way to get rid of a bad habit is to replace it with a good habit. For instance, if you are trying to get rid of the pridefulness in your life, then focus on creating a habit of humility. According to Scripture the opposite of humility is self-centered pride. Humility is not about putting yourself down; that's false humility. Humility is about lifting others up. If I am about *me*, I am selfish. If I am about *you*, I am humble. I really do think it's that simple.

One popular method for building habits is called the 21-90 rule. The idea is to commit to a new habit for twenty-one days. After three weeks of consistency, you'll have established it as a habit; then simply continue to do it for another ninety days.

You didn't create the bad habit overnight, so you aren't going to replace it overnight either.

Let's talk about some things you can do to break the bad habit of pride.

Own It

You cannot deal with any bad habit in your life until you first identify it and then acknowledge that it has become a problem for you. C. S. Lewis talked about acknowledging pride: "If anyone would like to acquire humility, I can, I think, tell him the first step. The first step is to realize that one is proud."[3]

So how do you know if you are self-centered? Ask yourself if these things are true in your life:

Do you often become defensive?
Do you blame everyone else for your problems?
Do you have a hard time cooperating with others at work?
Are your conversations usually about yourself?

Most people are either unaware they are self-centered or they are convinced it's not that big a deal. It's been said that pride is the only disease that makes everyone sick except the person who has it. You have to own it before you can do anything to get rid of it. What we might think is a minor issue can quickly grow into habitual behavior. And if self-centered pride has become a part of your life, then it is hurting your relationships with people as well as your relationship with God.

Steps to a Godly Habit

STEP 1: CONFESS IT

"Confess your sins to each other and pray for each other so that you may be healed" (James 5:16 NIV). Confessing our sins to the person we have offended is a big part of dealing with pride in our life. It's never easy to confess our sins because we have to first swallow our pride. It means admitting we were wrong or that we failed or that we know we hurt this person. And once we confess, it brings our sin out of the darkness and into the light. And once something is in the light, we are more likely to deal with it.

If someone is angry with you because of your self-centered behavior, then confessing to that person can open the door for healing in your relationship. It demonstrates to the person you've hurt that you are committed to change in your life. And that you want the arrogance and self-centered pride to be gone!

It's also important to confess to God. Confession is an act of humility, and continued confession will keep you humble before the Lord. It will remind you of your need for God's help. It will help you stay focused on him.

STEP 2: HUMBLE YOURSELF

Being humble does not mean you think less of yourself; it just means you think of yourself less. It's the journey from being a "me" person to becoming a "you" person.

I am reminded of a story I once heard about a little girl who was eating cotton candy when her father asked, "How can a little girl eat so much cotton candy?" She said, "Well, I'm much bigger on the inside than I am on the outside." Healthy humility helps us be a bigger person on the inside, which will in turn impact our actions on the outside. Conversely, pride leads you to pretend to be bigger on the *outside* than you are on the *inside.*

Paul explained that humility is the solution for self-centered pride. In Philippians 2:5–11, he said:

> You must have the same attitude that Christ Jesus had.
>
> Though he was God,
> he did not think of equality with God
> as something to cling to.
> Instead, he gave up his divine privileges;
> he took the humble position of a slave
> and was born as a human being.
> When he appeared in human form,
> he humbled himself in obedience to God
> and died a criminal's death on a cross.
> Therefore, God elevated him to the place of highest honor
> and gave him the name above all other names,
> that at the name of Jesus every knee should bow,
> in heaven and on earth and under the earth,
> and every tongue declare that Jesus Christ is Lord,
> to the glory of God the Father.

Paul's point is that if you want to know what real humility looks like, look at Jesus.

Every day of your life, pride tries to smother whatever shred of humility is in your heart, which is why you have to be intentional about growing this habit of humility.

STEP 3: SPEND TIME LISTENING TO THE THOUGHTS AND OPINIONS OF OTHERS

Do you ever find you're so self-absorbed that you don't really care about the thoughts or opinions of others? Do you get so impatient waiting on someone to finish their thought that you cut them off by talking right over the top of them? Or do you simultaneously look at your watch or phone and smile at others or eat chips while someone is trying to talk to you? And do you ever find yourself hijacking a conversation so that it becomes all about you?

These are all examples of self-centeredness. One of the best ways to break this habit of pride is to intentionally listen. The next time someone is talking to you, stop what you are doing, make eye contact, use facial expressions, and really listen. I don't mean think about what you are going to say next, but really focus on what that person is trying to communicate to you. And before you ever change the subject, contribute to the conversation by asking them related questions or offering advice without making it all about you.

The very act of listening is the antithesis of pride. It re-centers your focus outside yourself. When you truly listen to the opinions of others, you are saying that your thoughts are not the only ones that matter.

STEP 4: BE INTENTIONAL ABOUT ASKING OTHERS TO HELP YOU

When you have a need to control your environment or the people around you, it's a clear sign of self-centeredness. That need for control makes it hard to connect with others. You don't want to admit you are ever wrong or have ever made a mistake because it feels like you are giving up control.

Of course, humility is the antidote for pride, so one of the ways to get past this is to ask others for help. Asking for help acknowledges that there are others more capable than you or who might be better than you at certain things. It's humbly admitting that you don't have all the answers. And that is a good thing.

STEP 5: PRACTICE BEING GRATEFUL FOR ALL YOU HAVE

Do you often pat yourself on the back? Do you feel like you are better than everyone else? Do you feel like anything good that has happened in your life is because of your own efforts? When you put yourself up on a pedestal it makes it difficult for anyone to get close to you and will hurt all of your relationships, including your relationship with God.

One of the best ways to avoid pride is for you to show others sincere gratitude for all they have done. Gratitude keeps you humble, and humility makes it impossible to feel proud. When you express thanksgiving to God for all that he has done in your life it takes the focus off yourself. When you show gratitude to your coworkers, it's impossible to take all of the credit. Gratitude is the key to doing away with pride. So practice being grateful for all those who are important in your life.

STEP 6: CELEBRATE THE GOOD THAT HAPPENS TO OTHERS AROUND YOU

If a coworker gets a promotion, be legitimately happy for him. If a friend wins an award, take her to lunch to celebrate.

My wife, Sandy, is so good at celebrating others. Not only is she good at it, she genuinely loves to do it. When our kids would get a good grade or do well in a music recital, she would fix their favorite meal for dinner and put up streamers and balloons with posters around the room saying, "You are a winner" or "I'm so proud of you." If one of her friends has something special happen in their life, Sandy will get all her girlfriends together to celebrate. She takes to heart the instructions to "rejoice with those who rejoice" (Rom. 12:15 NIV). The irony of celebrating others is that it will in turn make your own day feel pretty special.

Listen, friends, being a disciple of Christ is not about you. It's about him, and he wants us to serve others. In fact, let me just say it this way: If you are a Christian and life is still all about you, then self-centered pride has a grip on you. You have not discovered what it means to be a disciple of Christ.

If you are serious about breaking the habit of self-centeredness, then you need to replace it with a God-centered mentality, which means serving others first. And there is no better place to start than in your own home and among your own family. Find ways to serve those you love the most. If you are a parent, I would also look for serving opportunities that include your children so that you can model it for them. You want your kids to grow up thinking that's how they are supposed to live so they in turn will train their children in the same way.

Look for ways to serve your coworkers or neighbors. Several times throughout the years, if my neighbors were gone on vacation, I would cut their grass. The first time I did it, when the neighbor returned home, he asked my son if he should pay me. My son said, "No, I think he just wanted to help you out!" Also, look for ways you can serve at your church. Before I was a pastor, we were at the church all the time serving in various ways.

The point is to put some effort into being selfless. One of the ideas I had was to put five coins in one pocket and every time that I served a coworker, I would move one of the coins to the other pocket. My goal before the end of the day was to move all five coins over to the other pocket. Again, if you do it long enough, you create a habit of serving others. Another thing you can do is put reminders on your phone. Whatever you choose to use as a reminder, just look for ways to be intentional in serving the people around you.

The purpose of life has puzzled people for thousands of years. That's because we typically begin at the wrong starting point—ourselves. If you really want God's purpose fulfilled in your life, you have to start with God, not yourself. God never intended for us to have a self-centered mindset but instead a God-centered mindset. Just imagine what our world would be like if everyone was focused on God. Conflicts would disappear, strife would be banished, and jealousy would cease to exist. Think how your work environment would be changed. Backstabbing and gossiping would become things of the past. Office politics would be nonexistent. And think how the Church would change. No one would leave because of hurt feelings. It would be a place where everyone first thought about his brothers' or sisters' feelings. And it would be a place where everyone focused on God. I think the unchurched would come to a place like that in droves.

Friends, while you may not be able to completely change your church or your family or even your marriage by yourself, you *can* get rid of the self-centered pride in your own life. And once you have done that, I think you will be surprised at the impact your life will have.

I challenge you to be intentional about having a God-first mindset. Some might argue that this is not easy, and I would say they are right. It is hard to put the needs of others before your own. It is hard to put God's desires before your own. But once you completely submit to God, emptying yourself, kicking out your ego, then there will be room for God to breathe his Holy Spirit upon you and fill you with his love. Then you will come to realize and understand what being a disciple of Christ is really all about.

2

ANGER

Whatever is begun in anger, ends in shame.

—Benjamin Franklin

I grew up in a middle-class home with parents who loved me. And yet I had a father with a lot of unresolved anger. I never quite knew when he was going to blow or what might set him off. It could be anything from a teenager driving too fast up our street to our having the volume too loud on the television while he was trying to fall asleep at night. But whatever it was, when it happened, things would get loud and expletives would fly.

These outbursts of anger created a lot of different emotions for me as a child, everything from fear to embarrassment to anger. Yes, *his* anger made me angry. Once when I was about ten years old, I was playing out in the front yard with friends. My dad was working nearby on a lawnmower that wouldn't start. He grew so frustrated over this uncooperative lawnmower that he grabbed ahold of the handle and spun it around several times like a discus thrower, finally letting it fly off the side of an embankment. My friends all witnessed this and laughed hysterically. But to me it wasn't funny. I still remember the embarrassment I felt.

On another occasion when I was about eleven years old, he and I were in the car going somewhere. As we approached a stop sign, he was not paying attention and rear-ended the car stopped in front of us. Immediately he turned and began to yell at me for not warning him of the stopped car.

I now understand that something had obviously happened in my father's life, long before he got in the car that day. I don't mean minutes or hours before—I mean years before. Some injustice in his life that was totally unrelated to that fender bender. Whatever hurt or offense it was that was never resolved left him responding to every perceived injustice with anger. After awhile anger became so much a part of his life that he didn't even notice the damage it was doing to those he loved the most.

Now fortunately for me, this story ends on a much happier note. In my teenage years my dad discovered a relationship with Jesus Christ, which completely changed his life. From that moment on, he went out of his way to make sure I knew he was proud of me and that he loved me.

Not only did God become the most important thing in his life but serving God became a priority for him. Now I'm not telling you that he never became angry again, because like all of us, there were things that upset him. But I believe my father broke the habit of responding to every difficult or uncomfortable thing in his life with anger.

It is important to mention that anger is not always a bad thing. In fact, anger is a God-given emotion, and in its proper place can be a source of strength and protection. It's designed to help us deal with any threat that might come into our life. The problem isn't the anger itself but the loss of control of your words or your actions. For instance, we know that Jesus got angry on several occasions. One example is when merchants were turning religion into a moneymaking scam. Jesus confronted them and ran them out of the temple.

I believe there are a number of things that make Jesus angry. Racism angers God; injustice angers God. I think it angers God to see an adult harm a child, to see someone break their marriage vow and commit adultery. Friends, God is love and sometimes the loving thing to do is to get angry. And even though Jesus got angry, Scripture clearly tells us that he never sinned.

So, the type of anger that Jesus demonstrated was more of a righteous indignation. He got angry at those who acted contrary to God's standard of fairness, justice, and goodness. This anger is more directed to the *wrong* that was done and not so much toward the *person* involved.

In fact, anger has produced great movements, such as MADD, Mothers Against Drunk Driving. Their anger over the loss of their children motivated them to do something about it by starting one of the largest victim advocate groups in America.

But on the other hand, anger is an emotion many of us experience when things in our world are not going the way we want them to. When you have been working toward a promotion, but it goes to someone else. When you tell your kids to clean their room, but they ignore you. When you have been waiting in a doctor's office long after your appointment time.

But if anger becomes your response every time you don't like something, it will become a habit. And if you start to accept that anger habit as normal, it will eventually control your life and keep you from experiencing God's best. It also has the potential to hurt your health, wreck your peace of mind, destroy your relationships, and even threaten your career—my father lost several jobs because of his anger issues—which is why it's important not to ignore a habit of anger in our lives.

I once heard psychologist and author Dr. Richard Dobbins speak to a group of men at a conference. He said that men typically have three issues they struggle with in life:

1. sexual issues,
2. anger issues, and
3. lying about both of the above.

Anger is often what fuels sexual lust. For instance, the #MeToo Movement is a social movement against sexual harassment that advocates for females who have experienced various forms of sexual violence to speak out about their experience. We often blame rape, or any form of sexual misconduct against women, on sexual lust when, in reality, it's more often caused by a man's unaddressed struggle with anger. It's anger that fuels the lust that leads to feelings of inadequacy and shame that then fuel even more anger. That is why our goal should not be so much anger management as it is to completely eradicate this habit from our lives.

Anger has become a public epidemic in America. You see the signs of our nation's irritability everywhere you go. Think about the polarization of our political system, the everyday nastiness of the online world, the workplace or school shootings. It's so bad that we are afraid to lock eyes with anyone in fear they might lose their cool and pull out a gun. It is an angry world that we are living in.

And yet most violence in America is not random. For instance, roughly 80 percent of murders reported to the FBI (in which the victim-offender relationship was known) were committed by friends, loved ones, or acquaintances.[1]

According to the National Domestic Violence Hotline, more than twelve million men and women are abused each year in the US by an intimate partner. The American Society for the Positive Care of Children says that more than 4.1 million child abuse cases are reported annually. Many of those are committed by an angry, out-of-control parent.[2]

A study led by researchers from Harvard Medical School found that nearly two-thirds of US adolescents have experienced their own anger attack that involved threatening violence, destroying property, or engaging in violence toward others at some point in their lives. These severe attacks of uncontrollable anger are much more common among adolescents than previously recognized.[3]

You can't help but wonder where all this anger is coming from in children. No one is born with these anger issues. Clearly, they learn it by copying the behavior of angry people around them. Maybe one or both parents berate and belittle family members. Maybe they see it at school with teachers or other students acting out on the playground. Maybe they witness it in some public situation or on the television. This is how a child grows up thinking that uncontrolled anger is normal behavior. And it's why, if you are a parent, you need to not only control your anger in front of your children but also explain to them how inappropriate uncontrolled anger is when they witness it in other settings.

Psychologists have called our generation "the age of rage." It's become so common we have created our own "rage" vocabulary.

For instance, *road rage* is a term I know you've heard, or possibly even experienced. Or maybe you have experienced "check-out rage" while waiting in a long line at a retail store. And it seems like everyone is addicted to their cell phones, which has led to "phone rage," where you get extremely angry while on the phone because you're unhappy with a product or service. Then there is "text rage," which is physical violence induced by a disparaging text. And then "on-hold rage," which is created by being put on hold for an infinite amount of time.

You can also see it in recreational activities such as "golf rage." Several years ago, I was playing golf with a friend who got upset over how badly he was playing. After one bad shot he got so upset that he threw his golf club into the pond. Later, once he cooled down, he went back and waded into the murky pond to retrieve his golf club. Proverbs 14:29 says, "People with understanding control their anger; a hot temper shows great foolishness." If you have ever seen anyone lose their temper or respond in anger you might have felt embarrassed for them because of how foolish they acted.

Yet there are some of you who might argue that you can't control your anger. And I would simply push back and say that while you might not be able to control your situation, or how it makes you feel, you certainly can control how you express your anger. It reminds me of the actor who was playing the part of Christ in an outdoor Passion play. As he carried the cross up the hill, a tourist began to heckle him, make fun of him, and shout insults at him.

Finally, the actor had taken all he could take. He put down his cross, walked over to the tourist, and punched him in the face. After the play was over, the director told him, "I know he was a pest, but I can't condone what you did. I mean you are playing the part of Jesus, and Jesus would have never retaliated. So, don't do that again." The actor promised he would control his temper and that it would never happen again.

But sure enough, the same heckler was back again the following day for the next performance. The actor tried to ignore him, but his anger got the best of him, and, again, he put down the cross and punched the guy in the nose. The director said, "That's it. We cannot have you behaving this way while playing the part of Jesus."

The actor begged, "Please just give me one more chance. I need this job, and I can handle it if it happens again." The director decided to give him one more chance. The next day the actor was carrying his cross up the road again. And sure enough, that same heckler was back. The actor was really trying to control himself. He was clinching his fists and grinding his teeth. Finally, still carrying the cross, he pointed his finger toward the heckler and said, "I'll meet you after the resurrection!"

When we don't control our anger, we sure don't seem much like Jesus.

One pastor said we act like a skunk; we spray our stinking temper on anyone who gets in our way. Some of us use anger to motivate people to action. You yell at your kids to motivate their behavior. You yell at a salesclerk to motivate her to help you. You yell at your employees to make them work harder. And it works! At least in the short term. You can scare people into doing almost anything. But in the long run, you will always lose, because anger always alienates people. Think about it: When people are angry and shouting at you, does that draw you closer to them or push you away from them?

If you are a parent and you are using anger to try to motivate your kids, you are pushing them away. When your kids are young, they think you are a superhero. Everyone else might think you are quirky or odd, but not your kids—they think you can do no wrong. Their spirits are wide open to you, but if you continue to show anger toward them, they will shut down. Even if you show them love at other times, they will build a wall to try and protect themselves from the unexpected outbursts of anger. Paul recognized this danger when he warned, "Fathers, do not provoke your children to anger by the way you treat them. Rather, bring them up with the discipline and instruction that comes from the Lord" (Eph. 6:4).

If you do struggle with anger you may feel like there's nothing you can do about it. But I will tell you that you have more control over your anger than you think. You *can* learn to express your emotions without losing control. If you don't think you are able to, then get professional help from a Christian counselor who has experience working with anger issues. Because, if you don't, you risk losing a relationship with the people you love the most.

So let's look at how to break this habit of anger in your life.

Own It

Oftentimes we justify our outbursts of anger. We excuse ourselves by blaming others for our anger. "It's those kids of mine." "It's my coworkers who make me so mad." "If she wouldn't have said that, I wouldn't have lost my temper." If we are serious about getting rid of this habit of anger in our lives, we have to stop blaming others and own it. "People who conceal their sins will not prosper, but if they confess and turn from them, they will receive mercy" (Prov. 28:13).

I would encourage you to go to the people who have been victim to your anger and own it with them. For instance, say to your kids, "I have demonstrated way too much anger with you. I want you to know I am going to work on it. Would you please forgive me?" You will make so much headway in repairing the relationship with your kids when you own it. With your spouse, with your coworkers, with your friends. When you swallow your pride and own it, you will begin to repair those relationships. You are the only one who can deal with your anger. But that will not happen until you first identify and acknowledge that it is a problem in your life.

Steps to a Godly Habit

STEP 1: IDENTIFY THE SOURCE OF YOUR ANGER

If you are in the habit of losing control of your temper over every perceived injustice in your life, then you need to figure out what's behind that anger. This might surprise you, but the immediate object of your anger is usually not the primary problem. Once you understand what's behind your anger, you are more likely to resolve it.

For instance, when someone criticizes you, why do you become angry or get defensive? Possibly because of your insecurity of not feeling like you measure up. Physical or emotional pain can also cause anger. For example, when I was younger, I had a lot of unexplained joint pain. I found that I was more impatient with people and quick to lose my cool because I was in physical pain. Maybe someone deeply hurt your feelings or broke your heart, and now you are quick to lash out at others who had nothing to do with that incident.

Sometimes your anger comes from a place of personal disappointment because you are not where you want to be at this stage of your life. And while it makes you feel angry at yourself, you respond to others out of your own disappointment.

I would also point out that unhealthy relationships are a very common cause for anger. Things are not going well in your home life, so your anger easily rises in unpredictable and unexpected ways.

If you can identify the source of your anger, you are more likely to understand how to deal with it.

STEP 2: LEARN TO CALM DOWN BEFORE YOU REACT

When you start to feel anger rising up, take a few minutes to calm down, to step away and collect your thoughts. Self-talk can be so effective. Ask yourself: "Is it really worth getting this upset? Will my anger really solve anything?" If your kids cause you to get angry, stepping away for a moment can prevent an overreaction. Say, "I'll be back in a little while and then we are going to talk about this." Go for a walk, a drive, or just into the other room until your emotions stabilize. Then go back and talk about their behavior in a calm way.

The same goes for your marriage. You cannot talk with your spouse when you are angry. There might be a lot of words going back and forth, but you are not communicating because those angry emotions have created a wall a mile high between the two of you. You are wasting your time trying to resolve your problems while angry. Proverbs 29:11 says, "Fools give full vent to their rage, but the wise bring calm in the end" (NIV).

The point is to take some time and have a little talk with yourself before you act or speak. Put your mind in gear before you put your mouth in motion. I once heard someone say, "I've never regretted silence, but I've often regretted what I spoke." James tells us, "Understand this, my dear brothers and sisters: You must all be quick to listen, slow to speak, and slow to get angry" (James 1:19).

Often it takes only a minute of self-talk to do the trick. And one of the best ways to bring everything back into perspective is to remind yourself that God's Word is full of promises. For instance, you might think, "I know this situation is frustrating, and yet I also know that Scripture tells me that God is in control." "We know that God causes everything to work together for the good of those who love God and are called according to his purpose for them" (Rom. 8:28).

Once you have calmed yourself down through self-talk, you should also go and calmly talk to the person who has offended you. You see, here's the problem with anger: If you get angry with me, my natural reaction is to get angry right back at you. But if you come to me in sincerity and say, "Man, that really hurt when you said that. Can we talk about it for a minute?" You are more likely to get a sympathetic audience. The point is, if you learn to control your tongue, you will control the damaging effects of your anger. Your anger is a threat to the life of peace that God desires for you, and that's why it's important to calm down before you react.

STEP 3: GET SOME EXERCISE

Physical activity can help reduce the stress that causes you to get angry. So yes, it does help to take a walk, go to the gym, ride a bike, or whatever you need to do to reduce your anger and stress level. Doing something physical is one of the most effective ways to reduce your anger. Exercise will also release endorphins in your body, which will help you to feel better and reduce your level of stress.

A MentalHelp.net article states:

> The American College of Sports Medicine's fifty-seventh annual meeting in Baltimore discovered that exercise might have a beneficial effect on anger in men.
>
> It is important to remember that if you are a person who easily gets angry and has angry outbursts, you could be harming your health. This chronic expression of anger gives rise to cardiovascular disease. So if you want to better manage your angry feelings when they arise, a good workout may be the way to go.[4]

STEP 4: LET GO OF ANGER CORRECTLY

In other words, now that you are reflecting on your emotions, decide to handle your anger in healthy ways. Here are some ways you might be repressing your anger:

- You keep yourself busy, so you have no time to feel.
- You live with a low-grade level of depression. Some have said depression is actually anger turned inward.
- You are sarcastic. You think you are so witty with your sarcasm, but it actually stems from repressed anger. Somebody once said a sharp tongue will cut your own throat.
- You allow little things to bother you.
- You suffer from a lot of muscle tension or fatigue.
- You have nervous habits like biting your nails or picking at your skin.

- You struggle with addictive behavior or you are passive-aggressive.
- You have a vindictive spirit and take the approach, "I don't get mad, I just get even."

All of these things come from repressed anger, and they are not healthy and will eventually damage your relationships.

When you repress your anger, you not only bottle it up inside, but you're not even aware it's there. In fact, if someone pointed out any of these areas and asked you if you were angry, you would deny that you are. If practiced for a long enough period of time, repressed anger can cause deep anguish that can bring on emotional as well as physical disorders.

Again, my friends, anger will always find an expression. You will either complain, blame, or criticize, but your anger will always find release. People who are often critical about their church or their kid's school, or about things at work or with their spouse, are often people who are simply trying to repress their anger.

Something hurt them or frustrated them, but instead of dealing with the issue, they have tried to repress it. What they need to do is go back and address the hurt in their life.

What's unfortunate is that many Christians mistakenly assume that repressing their anger is the biblical way to handle it. It is not! As I mentioned earlier, there is another word for repressed anger, and that word would be *depression*. I've certainly recognized it at times in my own life. What about you—are you struggling with low-grade depression? If so, then all the more reason to let go of harboring your anger.

One more thing I want to mention is to not express anger in an unhealthy manner. This is often seen in violent reactions, outbursts, put-downs, and physical abuse. A person like this often leaves burn marks on everyone in their path. Some of you might express your anger by getting even, holding a grudge, pouting, or being mean. Even when you don't verbalize your anger, everyone around you is very much aware that you are angry. They can see it in your facial expressions as well as your body language.

If I'm being blunt, some people just need to grow up. It takes maturity to manage our anger. You're not going to get better on your own. You need God's help to resolve the hurts and frustration in your life; you need God's help to get rid of the insecurities and fears. Colossians 3:15 says, "Let the peace of Christ *rule* in your hearts" (NIV, emphasis mine). There lies the secret to overcoming anger: God's power can change your life when you decide to let the peace of Christ rule in your life instead of allowing anger to rule. God wants you to experience his peace and his joy, but you have to be intentional about moving in that direction instead of toward anger.

STEP 5: PRACTICE FORGIVENESS

Jesus was unjustly beaten and mocked. They placed a crown of thorns on his head, and they nailed his hands and feet to a wooden cross. If anyone had the right to be angry, it was Jesus. And yet, at the very pinnacle of his suffering, do you remember what he said? "Father, forgive them, for they don't know what they are doing" (Luke 23:34). If you really want to get rid of your anger, you must choose to forgive the person who has done you wrong.

I have heard it said, "Not forgiving is like drinking rat poison and then waiting for the rat to die."[5] Forgiveness is something that everyone encourages us to do, but most of us have a hard time doing it. Paul summed it up well: "Make allowance for each other's faults, and forgive anyone who offends you. Remember, the Lord forgave you, so you must forgive others" (Col. 3:13).

We are all fallen people. We're going to do and say things that will be hurtful to others, even if unintentionally. When we are on the receiving end, we need to be willing to let it go, which is why forgiveness has more to do with our own spiritual maturity than it does the person we are forgiving.

Late author and theologian Lewis Smedes once said, "To forgive is to set a prisoner free and discover that the prisoner was you."[6]

And yet forgiveness is a choice you keep making day after day. You don't simply say "I forgive you" one time and magically the anger and resentment are gone. It's not easy. True forgiveness requires an attitude that says, "I let this go yesterday, and I am going to lay it down again today, and I am going to lay it down again tomorrow and the next day and the day after that." You must be intentional and determined that you are going to continue to let go of this bitterness until it is gone once and for all. Don't be afraid to ask God for his help, and as you continue to let this go, it will dissolve over time. Forgiveness is one of the most powerful and healing tools we have.

STEP 6: GIVE YOUR ANGER AN EXPIRATION DATE

"And 'don't sin by letting anger control you.' Don't let the sun go down while you are still angry" (Eph. 4:26). How do you let anger control you? By not dealing with it! Paul said to resolve your anger before the sun goes down. In other words, don't let a day pass without resolving your anger. To do that you must decide to keep short accounts. "I am angry with this person, but before this day is over, I am going to let it go." When you allow angry emotions to accumulate, like a pressure cooker, they have the potential to explode in destructive and inappropriate ways that will only hurt people and leave you with regrets.

STEP 7: RELY ON GOD'S HELP

If you really believe that God has a plan for your life, you will experience contentment and peace rather than anger when things don't go your way. You didn't get that promotion, so you want to get angry. But then you realize God has a plan for your life. He sees what you don't see, and he loves you. You may not fully understand what he is doing, but you trust him, so there is no reason to get upset.

Anger is not something you can prevent, but as long as you keep your anger under control, you will have more peace and healthier relationships.

3

EXCUSES

> He that is good for making excuses
> is seldom good for anything else.
>
> —Benjamin Franklin

I have felt like I was supposed to be an author for as long as I can remember. Before I was in pastoral ministry, I was a financial planner. I had an idea for a book on investing made easy, but every time I started writing down my thoughts, I came up with all kinds of excuses as to why it wasn't the right time. I would tell myself I wasn't quite knowledgeable enough. Or I would look at other investment books and tell myself I didn't have the credibility that all those other famous authors had. All of my excuses were rooted in my fears and insecurities, but they were enough to make me abandon the project multiple times.

Several years later, I left the financial planning world and went into full-time pastoral ministry. After a few years, I once again started to feel like I wanted to write. I even attended a few seminars on how to write a book. I would preach a sermon series and tell myself that with some effort it could be a book. I would start to work on the project, but then it would happen again—the excuses would begin to flow.

Throughout my thirty years of ministry I have started and discarded over a dozen books. I have had many friends try to encourage me to write, but they were never able to overcome my excuses.

"What do I know about writing a book?"

"What do I have to say that hasn't already been said a million times before?"

"I am pastoring a rapidly growing church. I just don't have time to write a book."

But again, those excuses were rooted in my own fears and insecurities. I was afraid no publisher would be interested in what I might write. I was afraid that even if a publisher did want to publish it, no one would want to buy it.

We all make excuses. We rationalize why we didn't follow through with our commitment, stick to the plan, or chase our dreams. And, yes, it can become a habit. Maybe you know someone who always has a ready excuse. Maybe you are that person! If so, it's time for that habit to be broken, and there is no reason why you can't start today.

As a pastor I can relate to what author and pastor Calvin Miller once said in an article about his call into ministry:

> I was so inferior even the neighbors noted it and pointed it out to my mother as I grew up. In my late teens, one of my sisters felt led of God to help me get in touch with myself by telling me that in her opinion, which was as inerrant as the

King James Bible, that if God called me to do anything, he must have had a wrong number. When I told my preacher I was called to preach, he didn't necessarily feel that God had a wrong number, but he was concerned that I might have had a poor connection.[1]

I suspect most of us have become skillful at picking from a wide range of excuses to limit our own capabilities. And that can be true in every area of life from going to the gym to studying for an exam to losing weight. Have you heard any of these common excuses?

"There's simply not enough time in the day to get it all done."
"It's just not the right time."
"I don't make enough money to be successful."
"I'm too old to change."

Have you used any of these before? I'm pretty good at coming up with excuses. Here is one that usually works well: "I just don't feel good."

We also come up with a lot of excuses for not serving God:

"I'm a new Christian."
"It's the preacher's job."
"That's not my spiritual gift."
"I haven't prayed about it."
"I am just too busy right now."

Listen, there are no good reasons for not obeying the Lord, only excuses. What is God asking you to do? He is asking you to step out in faith and trust him. Excuses are a waste of your time and they won't fix your problems. In fact, they will hold you back from your potential. Jim Rohn, a popular motivational speaker, once said, "If you really want to do something, you'll find a way. If you don't, you'll find an excuse."[2]

An excuse is simply a rationalization for the shortcomings in your life. Excuses place blame on an external problem for what is more than likely an internal condition. In other words, the reason I'm making the excuse is because of my own internal battle with fear or embarrassment or uncertainty or even success! All of these things (and many others) can cause you to derail your dreams or limit yourself at best. I think I can safely say that making excuses is one of the biggest reasons people are unable to accomplish what they want in life.

Several famous people have made remarks about excuses.

George Washington Carver once said, "Ninety nine percent of the failures come from people who have the habit of making excuses."[3]

Laura Schlessinger once said, "People with integrity do what they say they are going to do. Others have excuses."[4]

Gabriel Meurier said, "He who excuses himself, accuses himself."[5]

So then why do we feel the need to make excuses? Well, there are a lot of reasons, but I believe the number one reason is because of our fear. Fear can paralyze you and keep you from moving too far outside your comfort zone. That's why I believe facts are your friends. The more you educate yourself about the situation or the process, the easier it is to overcome those fears.

Fear of the unknown is very common. You start to worry about what might happen. You find yourself saying, "But what if?" and it paralyzes you from moving forward. And so you make excuses to cover your lack of progress.

Or maybe you fear failure, so you give up before you even get started. Listen, it doesn't matter how talented you are, whenever you attempt anything new there is always the possibility that you will fail. But even if you do, it can be an opportunity to learn and grow. Just because you attempt something and fail does not mean you are a failure. I would much rather make an attempt at my dreams and miss than never try and end up with all kinds of regrets.

Another common reason for making excuses is a lack of motivation. You need motivation for everything from dieting to studying to making home repairs. If you don't have it, you'll procrastinate and make excuses and always be stuck right where you are.

Motivation doesn't just fall from the sky and hit you in the face. If you want to get rid of your apathy you have to take some steps to build motivation in your life. If you don't challenge yourself, it will prevent you from growing.

Or it could be that you simply have a stubborn streak. You are so set in your ways that you don't want to make the changes, so instead you make excuses as to why you won't change. The root of stubbornness is the fear of letting go of your own ideas or convictions. If stubbornness is your reason for making excuses, then I would encourage you to be open to setting aside your ideas for other possibilities.

You will also find it easy to make excuses when you don't have any specific goal. For instance, "I want to get in shape this year" is a fuzzy, nonspecific goal. "I am going to go to the gym three times each week" is a very specific goal. If you don't have a specific goal, you will not reach it and will be forced to make excuses to explain why.

The last one I will mention is your belief that you are ill-equipped to accomplish the task. For instance, you may love to serve at church, but you don't feel like you are gifted enough. Or you would love to go back to school, but you don't think you're smart enough. Or you would love to apply for that promotion, but you don't think you're young enough.

What do you need to do to put an end to this habit of excuse-making? Let's look at ways to help you take responsibility and eliminate all excuses for good.

Own It

We have an incredible ability to make excuses. But it's one of the most destructive habits in our life, which is why we need to take the necessary steps to stop. If your employer is someone who lets you get by with making excuses or if you are married to someone who blindly accepts your excuses or if your landlord just accepts your excuses for late payment every month, all of these folks are doing you a tremendous disservice. You might even start to believe your own excuses. But they are keeping you from taking responsibility for your shortcomings.

It's time to acknowledge that making excuses is keeping you from accomplishing all that God wants you to accomplish. While you might not be able to change your circumstances, you can certainly change the way you respond, by taking the steps necessary to fulfill your responsibilities and your obligations.

Some people spend more time coming up with an excuse

than they do trying to complete the task. These excuses will only hijack your God-given potential and leave you short of God's plan for your life.

Steps to a Godly Habit

STEP 1: REPLACE YOUR FEARS WITH FAITH

When fear becomes your initial response to most situations, it can hold you back and leave you in an endless cycle of procrastination. We've talked about the fear of failure and the fear of the unknown. There are other things that might intimidate you, such as the fear of embarrassment, the fear of change, the fear of taking responsibility, or even the fear of success! Fear will cause us to settle for less than God's best.

Faith, on the other hand, is the opposite of fear. Hebrews 11:1 describes faith as "the assurance of things hoped for, the conviction of things not seen" (ESV). Although we cannot physically see God, we know that he is present and working in our lives. Faith can deliver us from our fears.

Hebrews 11:6 says, "And it is impossible to please God without faith." It doesn't say it is hard to please God; it says without faith it is impossible. While *faith* focuses on God, *fear* focuses on the problem. While *faith* is trusting and believing God, *fear* is to not trust him, to doubt that he even cares. And therefore, we feel the need to justify or make excuses for our life in an attempt to boost our own self-esteem.

Faith is a gift that God has given every believer. And God wants our faith to grow. Scripture instructs us on how to develop a faith that will conquer our fears. Romans 10:17 says, "Faith comes from hearing, and hearing through the word of Christ" (ESV). If you want to build your faith, then you need to study the Word of God. The Word of God is like an instruction manual for the Christian. If you really want to know God and to rely on his direction for your life, then you must read his instruction manual.

Another thing that's important to build faith in your life is to spend time with God in prayer and worship. When David, a psalmist, was afraid, he said in response to God, "When I am afraid, I put my trust in you" (Ps. 56:3 NIV). Prayer is one of the greatest privileges God has given us. It's easy for the struggles of life to get our attention. But when we pray it refocuses our attention back on God. It allows God to develop and grow our faith so that our dependence is on him.

God loves you and wants the best for you, so decide you are going to replace your fear with faith in God's plan for your life.

STEP 2: STOP BLAMING OTHERS

Whether it's fear of criticism, negative consequences, or attention, we don't want to feel bad, so often we blame someone else. I am reminded of a story I read a few years back about a girl named Jazlyn who loved McDonald's. On a regular basis she would have a McMuffin in the morning and a Big Mac meal with an apple pie in the evening.

Ashley, on the other hand, was more of a Happy Meal girl. While Jazlyn was nineteen years old, five foot six, and 270 pounds, Ashley was fourteen years old, four foot ten, and 170 pounds.

The two teenagers sued the McDonald's Corporation as well as the two stores they frequented in the Bronx for damages related to their obesity. They claimed McDonald's was responsible for their obesity because the restaurant chain did not provide the necessary information about the health risks associated with their meals.[6]

Making excuses by blaming others is not a new problem. We see it started clear back in the garden of Eden. The first man, Adam, said to God, "It was the woman you gave me who gave me the fruit, and I ate it" (Gen. 3:12). So the first man blamed the first woman, who blamed the serpent (and the poor serpent didn't have a leg to stand on).

In all seriousness, not only did Adam blame his wife but he extended the blame to God. He implied that he would have remained innocent if God hadn't put Eve in the garden with him. You and I can be guilty of doing that same blame-shifting that started clear back in the garden.

Blaming others might make you feel better in the moment. It might even take a little heat off you temporarily. But it never benefits you in the long run because eventually the people around you see the truth. People who play the blame game are generally very transparent. They think they're fooling people, but they're not.

STEP 3: STOP SAYING "I CAN'T"

In Jeremiah 1, God told Jeremiah that he was calling him to be a prophet to the nations. But Jeremiah said, "I can't speak for you! I'm too young!" (v. 6). God had a plan for Jeremiah's life, but immediately Jeremiah started making excuses. It's not that he *couldn't* speak for the Lord; it's that he *wouldn't* speak for the Lord. While these two words may appear to be similar, they are a world apart in meaning. For instance, do you ever say things like:

"I can't stop overeating."
"I can't find the time to pray."

"I can't communicate with my wife."
"I can't discipline my kids."

If you're honest, you know these statements are not true. They are no more than weak excuses. What we need to do is change our can'ts to won'ts.

"I won't stop overeating."
"I won't find the time to pray."
"I won't communicate with my wife."
"I won't discipline my kids."

The Lord pushed back on Jeremiah's can'ts and said, "Don't say, 'I'm too young,' for you must go wherever I send you and say whatever I tell you" (v. 7). Friends, when it comes to challenges, don't ever say you can't, because Scripture says, "I can do everything through Christ, who gives me strength" (Phil. 4:13). God will never ask you to do anything he won't first give you the ability to carry out.

STEP 4: DON'T FOCUS ON YOUR WEAKNESS, BUT FOCUS ON GOD

We all have areas of weakness. In Exodus 4 we see God giving Moses his marching orders. Moses was to go to Pharaoh and tell him to let God's people go. God then told him that he would perform miraculous signs through him. But Moses was letting fear get in the way and he started to make excuses. Exodus 4:10 says, "Moses pleaded with the Lord, 'O Lord, I'm not very good with words. I never have been, and I'm not now, even though you have spoken to me. I get tongue-tied, and my words get tangled.'"

Moses was focused on his own weakness when he needed to be focused on God's power to perform the miraculous.

We can do the same thing. Let's say you are trying to lose weight and you say, "My parents were both heavy, so I certainly won't be able to lose weight." Instead of focusing on your weakness, decide to focus on God. "I can do all things through Christ who gives me strength. With God's help I can lose that weight."

Or let's say you have a lot of debt, so you say, "I'm just not good with money, so I guess I will always be in debt." Instead of focusing on your weakness, focus on God. "God is teaching me to be faithful with all that he has entrusted to me. So I'm going to stop making excuses and take the necessary steps to be debt free." Jesus said in Luke 16:10, "If you are faithful in little things, you will be faithful in large ones. But if you are dishonest in little things, you won't be honest with greater responsibilities."

Listen, when you start to feel bad about yourself and start sliding into the dungeon of despair, when you are tempted to make excuses, just remember that you are created in the image of God. He has a grand design for you and good works that he planned in advance for you to do. Paul wrote in Ephesians 2:10: "For we are God's masterpiece. He has created us anew in Christ Jesus, so we can do the good things he planned for us long ago."

STEP 5: TAKE ACTION STEPS EVERY DAY

"What good is it, dear brothers and sisters, if you say you have faith but don't show it by your actions?" (James 2:14). Faith is a verb. It's action. It's doing. I know it can be a bit scary, but if it wasn't scary, would it really be faith? Decide each day of your life you are going to demonstrate your trust in God by taking a step toward your dreams, toward God's plan for your life. The only way you will ever eliminate your excuses is by taking some small steps forward each and every day. For instance, maybe you want to lose twenty-six pounds this year. Well, why not start with a small goal of losing a half a pound a week? You get the idea.

Successful people take action. They don't sit around making excuses, and they have the courage to achieve all that God has for them. I want you to know that you have the power to change. You may not think you do, but you do. If you can just embrace this truth, you've won half the battle.

But be ready. As soon as you decide to do away with excuses, Satan will flood your mind with one hundred reasons why you don't need to change or why you can't change. And when that happens, you have to be ready to ignore those lies and stand on the simple truth that the same power that hung the sun, moon, and stars now resides in you. Paul wrote in Romans 8:11, "The Spirit of God, who raised Jesus from the dead, lives in you. And just as God raised Christ Jesus from the dead, he will give life to your mortal bodies by this same Spirit living within you." What we cannot do in our own strength, God can. This should be especially encouraging to you when it comes to breaking this habit of making excuses.

So, my friends, do you want a better marriage? Do you want to be in better physical condition? Do you want to get your finances in order? Do you want to be a better parent? Do you want to strengthen your walk with the Lord?

Then *stop* making excuses.

No, it won't be easy. If it were easy, then everyone would accomplish their goals. Success is reserved for those who are obedient to God's plan.

Listen, friends, there is no advantage in making excuses. God is very much aware of your inabilities and your weaknesses, and he will never ask you to do something that he won't first give you the ability to carry out. So decide you're going to trust God, because on the day you take that final breath and you stand before him, he is only interested in hearing how you were faithful in everything he asked you to do.

Many years ago, a lady in our church told me that the first thing she did each morning was to commit her day to the Lord. It inspired me to create the same habit in my life. So for the last twenty-five years, every morning when I first put my feet on the floor, I simply say, "God, this is the day that you have made and I commit to live it for you." Now, that certainly doesn't mean I will never fail, but it does start my day with my focus on God.

If you are going to stop making excuses, then stop thinking about it, quit praying about it, and as Nike says, just do it!

4

LUST

Love is the great conqueror of lust.

—C. S. Lewis

During my years as a financial planner, a friend had given me a lead on an older gentleman who lived out in the country. He warned me that this man was a bit of a recluse, but he also had a lot of money and no one was advising him on how to invest it. So early one morning I drove to the country in search of this man's farm. As I turned into his driveway, in front of me I saw a very small white frame house that was in need of some repair. It had not been painted in quite a while and the shrubs had overgrown the front porch. I was pretty sure the front door had not been opened in several years. A few hundred feet away sat a barn that was twice as big as the house and looked fairly new. In the driveway sat a brand-new pickup truck. In the country most people use the back door and since the front door was blocked off by the shrubs, that's where I headed. I knocked on the door and an older man who was tall, thin, and unshaven came to the door and asked what I wanted. I explained that a friend of his thought he might be interested in my financial services. He opened the door and invited me to step just inside.

As I did, I was immediately taken aback by the smell. From where I stood in the doorway, to my right, I could see the front room. The shades were pulled shut and a table lamp was on low. There were boxes, newspapers, and books stacked around the room and dirty clothes thrown over some of the furniture. As I glanced to my left, I had a view of the kitchen. And like the front room, there were newspapers, as well as canned goods and dirty dishes, stacked on the table and kitchen counters. I explained to the gentleman how I might be able to help him with his investment needs, but he was simply not interested. I thanked him for his time and turned and exited out the door. As I walked to my car, I actually felt relieved he didn't want my help. I don't know if I could have spent much more time in that house. As I drove away from his farm that day, I couldn't help but wonder how someone could tolerate such filthy conditions. And yet it does seem that when people live around garbage long enough, they no longer see it as a problem. In fact they often justify their way of life and actually begin to feel comfortable with it. I think the same thing is true when it comes to how we handle sexual lust.

There is an old adage in the computer world: Garbage in, garbage out. In other words, if you allow poor quality input, it will always produce faulty output. In the same way, if you allow lustful thoughts to come into your head, lustful actions will occur. You will then begin to justify your thought life and no longer see it as a problem. Galatians 5:16 says, "So I say, let the Holy Spirit guide your lives. Then you won't be doing what your sinful nature craves."

Basically, lust is an insatiable craving to gratify your fleshly desires by seeking to satisfy a legitimate desire in an illegitimate way. Or you could simply say lust is a strong desire, because that's what the word literally means. Lust is often defined as a passionate and overpowering desire or craving for either sexual activity or even power. In Scripture it is listed as one of the seven deadly sins because it has the power to destroy. We can lust for any number of things. For instance, we can lust for money or possessions, power or influence, even food. But what I want to look at in this chapter is what most people think of when they think of lust, and that is sexual lust.

As I have mentioned several times, I've struggled with all of the issues I cover in this book to one degree or another, which is why I have included them. Just because I'm a pastor does not mean that I'm shielded from temptation. We all face temptation in our lives. As one pastor said, "It's depressing to realize that most of us are like the rest of us." So I believe that most of us have struggled with lust to one degree or another and at one time or another. If lust has become a common struggle in your life, then you need to decide to take the necessary steps to deal with it before it becomes a compulsive bad habit. You will know it has become a bad habit when you continue to repeat it in spite of the threat of negative consequences.

Since we have defined what lust is, let me now tell you what it's *not*. It's not noticing someone's appearance. It's normal for a man to notice a beautiful woman or for a woman to notice a handsome man. I have heard it said that it's not the first look that gets us in trouble; it's the second and third that usually cause the problem. We move from noticing someone's beauty to fantasizing about what we would like to do with that person. It's letting our mind go to an unhealthy place that's the problem. Lust involves a choice and an act of our will. I once heard author John Maxwell define it this way: "Lust is a thought that I entertain, cherish, or hold on to, that if I did what I was thinking, it would clearly be sin."

Many people have bought into the age-old lie that "it's okay to look, but just don't touch." In other words, it's okay to stare at a man or woman with lustful thoughts because I'm not actually doing anything to them. You feel justified with your lustful thoughts because you assume no one knows what you are thinking anyway. Your spouse doesn't know; the person you are lusting after doesn't know; no one around you knows; so, whom are you really hurting anyway? But friends, you know it's wrong—and certainly God is aware. God knows your every move, your every glance, your every thought. He knows your heart!

Someone said that our thoughts are simply action in rehearsal. If you rehearse the idea of inappropriate actions in your mind over and over again, it's only a matter of time before you will act those things out. James 1:14–15 says, "But each person is tempted when they are dragged away by their own evil desire and enticed. Then, after desire has conceived, it gives birth to sin; and sin, when it is full-grown, gives birth to death" (NIV).

Friends, we give birth to sin when we start rationalizing our behavior. We are only excusing our behavior when we call flirting with that coworker innocent fun. We are only excusing our behavior when we say the swimsuit edition only comes out once a year. We are only excusing our behavior when we sprinkle our conversation with sexual innuendos. Author Chuck Swindoll once said:

> Lust is no respecter of persons. Whether by savage assault or subtle suggestion . . . its alluring voice can infiltrate the most

> intelligent mind and cause its victim to believe its lies and respond to its appeal. And beware—it never gives up . . . it never runs out of ideas. Bolt your front door and it'll rattle at the bedroom window, crawl into the living room through the TV screen, or wink at you out of a magazine in the den.[1]

Lust is not a new problem. Paul addressed it clear back in the first century: "Because of this, God gave them over to shameful lusts" (Rom. 1:26 NIV).

Like every other boy in the late 1960s, I loved to look at the pictures in *National Geographic* magazine. But my first introduction to pornography was in the seventh grade when a boy in my class found a picture in his father's dresser drawer and brought it to school. I can still remember the confused feelings it created in me. I felt guilt for looking at the picture and yet at the same time I felt a sexual rush. That same year another kid brought a romance novel to school and showed me several descriptive sections in the book. So there I was at the age of twelve, and I had experienced lust sparked by a visual as well as lust formed in my imagination.

If you are a parent, here is what I want you to consider: My experience was over fifty years ago. If you wanted to look at porn back then you had to go looking for it. Today kids don't have to go looking for it; it comes to them. From the lyrics of the most popular songs to the iPhone they carry in their pocket, pornography is everywhere. If you are a parent, I hope you will pay close attention to these alarming statistics. The Kaiser Family Foundation conducted a survey in 2001 and found among teens ages fifteen to seventeen, "Seventy percent have accidentally stumbled across pornography online."[2] Thirty-two percent "of teens admit to intentionally accessing nude or pornographic content online."[3]

The US Department of Justice said: "Never before in the history of telecommunications media in the United States has so much indecent (and obscene) material been so easily accessible by so many minors in so many American homes with so few restrictions."[4] Seriously, parents, you should not ignore this potential problem with your kids! Pornography is at their fingertips. And a hormonal body with a curious brain is primed and ready to be enticed.

In a 2014 study the *Journal of Sex Research* found that, in a given week, 46 percent of men and 16 percent of women ages eighteen to thirty-nine intentionally viewed pornography. The journal noted that the numbers were significantly higher than previously believed.[5] The National Council on Sexual Addiction and Compulsivity estimates that 6–8 percent of Americans are sex addicts, which accounts for 18 to 24 million people.[6] Of course, we try to justify and legitimize it all by calling it "adult entertainment." *Lust* or *pornography* just sounds and feels dirty or wrong, and yet *adult entertainment* sounds and feels much more sophisticated or clean.

Here's the thing about lust: First, it does not deliver what it promises. We would expect to experience psychic ecstasy, but instead we experience guilt, emptiness, and a sense of loneliness.

Second, and perhaps the most deceptive fact about lust, is that it has an insatiable appetite: the more you try to satisfy it, the more intense it becomes. A 2014 fMRI study from the Max Planck Institute revealed that habitual porn use may actually affect the brain. Repeated exposure to porn appeared to cause the brain's reward center, called the striatum, to be less and less responsive. In other words, the brain becomes desensitized, requiring more and more stimulation to achieve the same level of pleasure. This is similar to the way illicit drugs affect the brain.[7]

And third, studies have also shown that those who are involved in pornography admitted to reduced sexual activity in their own life. Even though they believed porn to provide satisfaction and fulfillment, they discovered the very opposite occurred. It negatively affects intimacy with their spouse.[8]

Lee Strobel said, "Pornography won't spice up your sex life. It will poison it. It introduces false comparisons."[9] The *New York Times* told the story of a thirty-four-year-old woman who discovered that her husband, a minister, had an online porn habit. She said, "How can I compete with hundreds of anonymous others who are now in our bed, in his head? Our bed is crowded with countless faceless strangers, where once we were intimate."[10] Another woman said:

> After I discovered his pornography use, I somehow felt responsible, ugly, ashamed, alone, and hopeless. Why would he look at another woman unless I wasn't pretty or sexy enough? I felt like a failure as a wife and lover. Now I know that wasn't true. When we got help, I found out his pornography use began long before our marriage, as far back as his youth. Not only was it not my fault but it had nothing to do with me at all. After much counseling, we both understand that he entered our marriage thinking it would cure his sex problems; it didn't. We're still together. We are living proof that a porn or sex addiction doesn't have to mean the end of your relationship.[11]

The fantasy world of pornography is like this big carnival pulling people in every day with promises of great thrills, only to place them on a lonely roller coaster of excitement and emptiness, arousal and anxiety. In fact, most of the people engaged in porn live with an overwhelming fear—fear that they will be exposed and feel shame.

Over the years I have had dozens of men and women come to me for help with their addiction to pornography. And I can tell you that every one of them had an overwhelming fear that people would find out. A fear that someone will see them for who they really are. They know they need to talk to someone, but what if they tell someone about their problem and that person breaks their confidence? They worry they will lose their marriage or even their job. Which is why most people try to keep it a secret.

Of course, I think it goes without saying that pornography will hurt your relationship with God. People who indulge in porn often feel the need to hide from God because of their shame and guilt. Every time they pray, they are reminded that what they are doing is wrong. So rather than feel the guilt, they pull back from prayer or church attendance, they harden their heart so as not to feel the conviction of the Holy Spirit. Friends, no matter what you've been involved with up to this point, God is waiting to help you back to a healthy relationship with him—as well as your spouse, if you are married. But to get there you've got to make a serious commitment to break this habit of lust in your life.

Look what Jesus had to say about it: "You have heard the commandment that says, 'You must not commit adultery.' But I say, anyone who even looks at a woman with lust has already committed adultery with her in his heart. So if your eye—even your good eye—causes you to lust, gouge it out and throw it away. It is better for you to lose one part of your body than for your whole body to be thrown into hell" (Matt. 5:27–29). Is there any question about what Jesus thinks about lust? Of course this is hyperbole. He doesn't mean for me to literally pluck out my eye as a punishment for my sin, but he does want us to do whatever it takes to break this bad habit of lust. He is not condemning our natural interest in the opposite sex. He is warning us that when we move from interest to active fantasizing about illicit sexual behavior, we have crossed the line.

Many Christians have read the restrictions about sexuality or heard a preacher pound the pulpit and talk about the evils of sex. Nothing could be further from the truth. Sex is a good thing—it's a God thing! God is the architect and designer of the sexual relationship, which is intended for a man and a woman in a monogamous marriage. He created it to be something that expresses your love for your spouse and connects you physically and emotionally as well as spiritually. And yet it is a very powerful desire in our life, which is why God placed guardrails or boundaries around it. If we step outside of his boundaries it can implode and create all kinds of pain in our lives.

Years ago I lived in St. Joseph, Missouri, which borders the Missouri River. On the other side of the river was a small community called Elwood, Kansas. In July 1993 it rained for several days and just wouldn't stop. There was so much water the levees on the Kansas side broke through, putting the entire town of twelve hundred people underwater. While no one lost their life, they all lost most of their earthly possessions, and it was devastating to those families. In the same way, sexual desire is like a great river that is rich and deep and powerful and yet very safe as long as it stays within its proper channel. But the moment that river overflows its banks, it becomes destructive.

Own It

When people can see my bad habits, I'm more likely to deal with them because either people will hold me accountable or I want people to think highly of me. But on the other hand, when you have a habit like lust, it's a heart issue, so no one can see it and it's easy to conceal. And therefore I'm less likely to do anything about it. And that's why it's so important to own it.

I think most of us have struggled at one time or another with sexual lust, so just be honest with yourself as to how much of a problem it really is. Most people are convinced it's not that big of a deal. We say things like, "I know it's a bad habit, but it's just not a problem for me."

It's easy to get blindsided when you don't ever recognize lust as a problem. When we let our guard down, what we think is a minor little issue can quickly grow into habitual behavior. Paul wrote in Ephesians 5:3, "But among you there must not be even a hint of sexual immorality, or of any kind of impurity, or of greed, because these are improper for God's holy people" (NIV). Did you notice he said there should not even be a *hint* of sexual immorality? What would you consider a hint? Well, certainly, I would think looking at a porn website or imagining what you would like to do to some attractive person, looking at the annual swimsuit edition or reading that erotic romance novel would be somewhere near a *hint* of sexual immorality! There is always the temptation to get as close to sin as we possibly can without actually committing a sin.

It reminds me of the wealthy couple who were hiring a chauffeur. It came down to three applicants. The wife called the men over to her balcony and pointed to a brick wall alongside the driveway. She said to the men, "I would like to know how close you think you can get to that wall without scratching my car." The first guy said he could get within a foot of the wall without damaging the car. The second guy said he was confident he could get within six inches without damaging the car. The third guy said, "It doesn't matter how close I can get because I'm going to stay as far away from that wall as I possibly can." The third guy understood the point was not how close you can get to the wall; the point was to protect the car. Friends, the same is true with lust. Instead of seeing how close you can get to it without sinning, decide you are going to do everything you can to protect your soul, to protect your integrity! Decide you are going to stay as far away from lust as you possibly can.

Let me give you five ways you can break this bad habit of lust in your life, because without a strategy it will eventually turn into a spiritual stronghold that can become very destructive.

Steps to a Godly Habit

STEP 1: ASSESS YOUR NEEDS

Are you trying to fill an emptiness in your life with something less than what God intended? Romans 15:13 says, "I pray that God, the source of hope, will fill you completely with joy and peace because you trust in him. Then you will overflow with confident hope through the power of the Holy Spirit." God intended for us to have an intimate relationship with him, and he is able to fill the empty places of our soul and to meet the needs in our life. The more we draw toward the presence of God in our life, the less that sexual lust will be a problem for us.

STEP 2: BE AWARE OF THE CONSEQUENCES

Look around: all of us know of people who have wrecked their lives because they ignored their problem of lust. I know two different pastors who ignored their struggle with lust and ended up in sexual sin. Not only did they lose their ministries, they lost their integrity as well. In the church I pastor I have seen several people end up in divorce simply because they ignored sexual lust in their lives and it grew into a habitual problem.

Listen, we serve a God who loves us and will certainly forgive us for the mistakes we make with our sexual integrity, but there will still be consequences for us as well as the people we love the most. And of course if you are a Christian, not only will you do great damage to your witness for Christ, but the sin will hurt the people you love, leave you guilt ridden, and could destroy your future plans! Seriously, is it really worth it?

The book of Job says, "I made a covenant with my eyes not to look lustfully at a young woman" (31:1 NIV). Have you made that kind of a promise to yourself? When you are enticed to stare longer than you should, or take that second or third look, just remind yourself that person is somebody's son or daughter or they are somebody's husband or wife.

Some of you might be saying, "Steve, I understand what you are saying, but I'm single, so it doesn't matter." Oh my goodness, friends—it does matter! Regardless whether you are single or married, lust is sin and it can cause you to sin in your heart. And if it does lead to sex outside of marriage, you have just done damage to your relationship with this person as well as your relationship with God.

STEP 3: AVOID OBVIOUS AREAS OF TEMPTATION

In other words, don't feed your lust. Decide you are going to get rid of the things that are tempting you. If you are tempted to click on that porn website, I would encourage you to put accountability software on all of your devices, including your smartphone. There are several software packages available today. Most will send an e-mail to a spouse or an accountability partner each day showing what you have been viewing online. There are also packages that filter or block certain websites. A few of the companies that offer these packages are Covenant Eyes, Ever Accountable, Accountable2You, Net Nanny, Lion, and OpenDNS.

A couple of years ago, as a precautionary measure, I had one installed on my computer, and I have them send an e-mail to my wife each day showing her what I have been viewing. It takes all the temptation away from me, knowing that if I click on that website, my wife will know it. (And then I would die! Because she would kill me.) I also think it's wise to put every computer out in a public setting. That gives everyone in the house accountability.

I would also encourage you to be careful what you watch on television, drop some subscriptions to magazines, and get rid of any pornography or romance novels that you might have hidden around the house. The bottom line is you must dispose of all sources of stimulation in your home or at work that provoke your lustful thoughts.

And then you should ask yourself what influence your friends have on you. If you're spending time with the wrong people, you'll end up doing the wrong things. It doesn't matter if you are male or female; if your friends joke about porn or how hot that girl or guy is or flirt with the opposite sex, they will influence you in a negative way. It might make you uncomfortable at first, but after a while you may begin to think it's cute, and before long you find yourself joining in.

You may think you are strong and don't need any of these safeguards. Paul wrote in 1 Corinthians 10:12, " So, if you think you are standing firm, be careful that you don't fall!" (NIV). There was a man in the Old Testament by the name of Joseph, who served in Potiphar's household. Potiphar's wife tried relentlessly to get Joseph to go to bed with her. His response was, "How then could I do such a wicked thing and sin against God?" (Gen. 39:9 NIV). I'm sure you can imagine what a temptation this was for him. She was a beautiful lady and he was a handsome young man. Do you know what Joseph did? He ran! She tried to pull him into her bed, and he ran. Sometimes the most courageous thing a Christian can do is run. That's why Paul said in 1 Corinthians 6:18, "Run from sexual sin! No other sin so clearly affects the body as this one does. For sexual immorality is a sin against your own body."

STEP 4: ACCEPT GODLY COUNSEL

It's important to find an accountability partner of the same sex. Someone who cares about you and whom you can trust. Someone who is not afraid to get in your face if they need to, to ask you the tough questions. Alcoholics Anonymous has a slogan that says, "You are only as sick as your secrets." A secret kept in the dark will grow like black mold, and it will destroy you. But once that secret has been exposed or brought out into the open, its destructive power is diminished. If we can find the courage to express our struggles to somebody else, we are much more likely to avoid those temptations and to heed their challenges. Here are some questions you and your accountability partner can ask each other on a regular basis:

- Has your interaction with the opposite sex been honoring to Christ this week?
- Did you overstep any lines?
- Have you been participating in anything that you know is sin?

The bottom line is, if you cannot break this habit of lust in your life, then for goodness' sake get professional help before it becomes a spiritual stronghold. And if you need to be a part of a group, consider joining a support group in your church. For instance, our church offers Every Man's Battle groups as well as groups for women with sexual integrity problems. If your church doesn't already offer one, then I would suggest you contact New Life, 800-NEW-LIFE (800-639-5433) or visit NewLife.com/EMB/New-Life-Groups. They offer information on how you can get connected with a group and kits that have everything you need to start one in your own church. They also offer Every Man's Battle Weekend, which might be of interest to you.

STEP 5: ALLOW GOD TO GIVE YOU THE VICTORY

Friends, don't lose heart over setbacks. It's easy to get discouraged and want to give up, but you didn't create this habit overnight, and you are not going to get rid of it overnight. It will take time and you will make some mistakes along the way. And when you do, just evaluate where you slipped up and put safeguards in place so you don't slip in that area again.

I think one of the most important things you can do to help get victory over lust is a daily time with God in prayer and in the Word. When I pray it refocuses my attention on God, so I become sensitive to the Holy Spirit's conviction in my life. If I'm spending time with God, it is easier to say no to temptation when it comes. "Finally, I confessed all my sins to you and stopped trying to hide my guilt. I said to myself, 'I will confess my rebellion to the Lord.' And you forgave me! All my guilt is gone" (Ps. 32:5). Do you know who wrote that Psalm? King David, who was undone by his lust for Bathsheba. His lust grew into sexual sin. He later repented of his sin and God forgave him, and eventually he became known as a man after God's heart. He still had to face consequences for his sin, but God forgave him and restored him, and God wants to do the same for you and for me.

I heard about a father who was watching from the kitchen window as his four-year-old son played in the sandbox. He noticed his son was getting very frustrated—so frustrated that he began to cry. So the father went outside to find out what was wrong. The little boy said he couldn't get a big rock out of the sandbox. The father said, "Have you used every bit of strength available to you?"

The little boy said, "Yes, but I still can't get it!"

The father said, "Well, you haven't asked me for help."

The boy then said, "Dad, would you help me?" And together they were able to lift the rock out of the sandbox.

Friends, I think it is extremely difficult to change a bad habit by willpower alone. But we have a heavenly Father who loves us and wants the best for us. I am not telling you it will be easy, but I am telling you with the help of friends and with the help of your Father you can get victory over this bad habit of lust in your life.

5

CYNICISM

A cynic is a man who knows the price of everything, and the value of nothing.

—Oscar Wilde

I spent the first twelve years of my adult life as an entrepreneur and small-business owner. I then decided to leave the business world to go into pastoral ministry. As I approached my first position as senior pastor, I did so with a great deal of excitement as well as a lot of unrealistic ideas and expectations of what ministry was really all about.

I looked forward to the different ways I would be able to help people, such as those who might need assistance with food, shelter, or even finances. We were a small church, so all of the requests came directly to me. I hadn't been in my role very long before I got my first call from a lady in need of money for groceries. After listening to her story, I wanted to help, so the church gave her money. A few days later I was warned by the local police department that the money was not going toward food; this woman was scamming churches around town. I was embarrassed that I had fallen for this woman's ruse and determined I would be more careful in the future.

It was just a few weeks later that I got a call from someone needing money for a surgery for their child. Because of my previous experience I asked more questions this time, but this person had their story down pretty good, and they were able to answer all my questions. But, once again, I later discovered that I had been scammed.

After a few years in ministry it became very clear that there were a number of people whose sole purpose was to scam churches and other benevolent organizations. Unfortunately, I found myself moving from the disappointment I felt after those first few times of being scammed to feeling disillusioned by the idea of helping anyone at all. My disillusionment then grew into outright cynicism.

Instead of thinking the best of the people calling for financial help, I started to become skeptical of all of them. And because of my growing cynicism, we stopped helping as many people as we had in the past.

While there are a lot of different attitudes and habits that can be destructive to your faith and joy, cynicism is certainly right at the top. It's contagious and, like a virus, it's easy to catch but hard to get rid of. It has a way of seeping into your thought life undetected and infecting your entire outlook.

Cynicism might not even be on your radar, but I'm certain there have been times in your life when you felt its force. If that's true, then you need to get rid of the stinkin' thinkin' that's derailing God's best for your life.

Once I recognized how cynical I had become, I realized it was time to turn our church's benevolence ministry over to someone else. I was then able to move past the cynicism, at least in that area of my life.

Cynicism is a posture you might take on in an effort to protect yourself. It's often triggered when you feel repeated disappointment. In my case, a whole string of con artists. Maybe you have had several coworkers let you down. Or several politicians you've trusted who have not kept their campaign promises. Cynicism can become an outlet for your frustration.

Cynicism is no respecter of persons. Everyone—regardless of age or gender or socioeconomic level—is susceptible to cynicism. It's toxic, it robs you of happiness, it's extremely contagious, and it certainly plagues our culture today.

YourDictionary.com defines cynicism in a very enlightening way: "An attitude of scornful or jaded negativity, especially a general distrust of the integrity or professed motives of others."[1] In other words, it's basically an attitude of constant distrust or disbelief toward the actions of others, even when there's no logical reason for it. And it can take a negative toll on family and friends. Why? Because it's birthed out of our own pain. And if we allow it to grow, not only will it leave us dazed, but it will destroy any hope of a brighter future.

In his book *A Praying Life*, Paul Miller wrote: "Cynicism is so pervasive that, at times, it feels like a presence. . . . Weariness and fear leave us feeling overwhelmed, unable to move. Cynicism leaves us doubting, unable to dream. The combination shuts down our hearts, and we just show up for life, going through the motions. . . . Cynicism is the air we breathe, and it is suffocating our hearts."[2]

You are not born a cynic. Cynicism is a learned behavior

and an acquired habit. Therefore it's a habit that can certainly be broken. As a child you were innocent and carefree; you believed the best about everyone. And yet psychologists tell us that cynicism can actually begin as early as the first or second grade. Even at that young age there are many reasons why kids may already show signs of skepticism, which can quickly lead to cynicism. Perhaps they have watched their parents fight and get divorced. They may have been abused by an adult. Maybe they have been raised without a father. They could have been bullied in school. Possibly they have spent too much time on social media.

Unfortunately, it only gets worse as we move into the reality of our twenties and thirties.

It could be that friends who were once important in your life have now forgotten all about you. Perhaps you've worked your tail off for a company only to be told they are downsizing and you are being laid off. Or possibly there was a time you went out of your way to help a friend going through a difficult time, only to have that same friend later tell you they didn't think you cared. Maybe you worked a lot of long hours on a project with another coworker who in the end took all the credit.

Those types of things are very painful, not because they don't matter to you but because they do! I think if you look around today you will see that cynicism has become the dominant spirit of our age. You see its fingerprints in just about every area of life, from the television networks as they talk about politics, to the politicians themselves as they slam the other party, to the angry comments you see on social media.

Cynical people are faultfinders. They are always questioning the motives of one person while finding something negative to say about another. Only God knows another person's heart and the Bible warns us against judging. It says in Romans 14 to stop passing judgment on one another.

I was once at a social event and tried to start a conversation with a woman there. No matter what I said to her she would come back with a cynical response. I said, "Isn't this a great event?" She said, "We all know in the end they just want our money." After a few more comments it wasn't hard to see that this woman struggled with cynicism.

Of course, when you are the one who is cynical, you tell yourself that you are just being "realistic." You have convinced yourself that you are the only one who can see what's really going on here, which leads to a self-righteous attitude.

For instance, maybe you have a friend who is getting married. You feel like the guy she is marrying is not good enough for her. Everyone else seems to like the guy, but you're not convinced. You believe he is a jerk, and it irks you that no one else can see it.

The Bible also gives us examples of cynicism. For instance, in the book of Jonah we see God tell Jonah to go and preach repentance to the people of Nineveh. Jonah demonstrated cynicism when he responded that he did not want to go because the Assyrians did not deserve God's forgiveness.

My favorite example of cynicism is found in John's gospel. Philip went looking for his friend, Nathanael, to tell him about Jesus. He said, "We have found the very person Moses and the prophets wrote about! His name is Jesus, the son of Joseph from Nazareth." Nathanael then said, "Nazareth! Can anything good come from Nazareth?" (John 1:45–46). His response overflowed with cynicism. But once Nathanael met Jesus, his cynicism melted away.

Cynicism can also become your defense mechanism. Maybe somebody hurt you deeply, so you decide you will never open yourself up to let anyone hurt you like that again. Or perhaps you were dating someone who betrayed you and so now you have become overcautious of anyone who may ask you out. Or maybe you get new neighbors and assume they will be as unfriendly as the family who lived there before. You no longer see people for who they are; you now see everyone as potential hurt. But more than likely it's your cynicism that's actually causing people to respond to you the way they do.

That attitude of distrust and disbelief will put people off and cause them to avoid being around you. Your past pain that brought on this cynicism has now become your present reality. And what might have started as self-preservation could soon morph into something more dangerous. As you become jaded, your hurt and fear cause you to harden your heart. You could even get to the place where you don't feel like you need friends anymore. They will just end up hurting you anyway, so what's the point?

After a while you unwittingly begin cultivating a life of hurt and loneliness. And when you close your heart to people, you will inevitably close your heart to God. It doesn't matter why you closed your heart or whom you closed your heart to; once your heart is closed, it is closed to all relationships.

I also find it interesting that a lot of cynics used to be optimists. You would never know it, but there was a time they were full of hope and enthusiasm. So what happened? How does a person go from being positive to cynical?

At times it can come from knowing too much. I know that's counterintuitive. We often hear things like, "Then you will know the truth, and the truth will set you free" (John 8:32 NIV). And yet while I believe that's true, the truth still hurts and can cause us to be cynical. For instance, Job 6:25 says, "How painful are honest words!" (NIV). King Solomon was said to be the wisest man who ever lived, and yet listen to what he said in Ecclesiastes 1:18: "The greater my wisdom, the greater my grief. To increase knowledge only increases sorrow."

Years ago I worked as an investment planner and shared an office with a guy who I later found out had embezzled money from his clients. When I discovered what he had done, I immediately confronted him by phone. He laughed and hung up on me. I never saw the guy again. I considered him to be a trusted friend. I had traveled with him on business trips, and he and his wife had been in our home several times to share a meal. He was gregarious and well-liked by many people. He was a leader in his church and professed to love God. But I discovered he was not at all whom he pretended to be. So yes, it was good to find out the truth about this guy, but it was also a very difficult experience in my life.

What I have discovered is that it doesn't matter whether you are in ministry or business, people are going to hurt you; people are going to let you down. What matters most is how you respond to those hurts because your response will determine your future. You can either forgive the person who hurt you, or you will likely become cynical.

When I came to pastor my current church, the previous pastor had just died from a three-year battle with ALS, what's often known as Lou Gehrig's disease. As you might imagine, this congregation was hurting from this loss. I remember my first weekend as their new pastor, a man approached me as I came off the platform and said, "That was the worst sermon I've ever heard in my life." Wow! There is an old saying that "hurt people hurt people." Here I was in a new church, and already I was being confronted with cynicism. But this time I decided that I was not going to allow this man's hurt to create cynicism in me.

Own It

You might have gone your entire life without realizing you are cynical. Oh, you have known you were a bit sarcastic, but you've always insisted you were just keeping things real. And yet you are starting to notice that you pick things apart and everyone seems to annoy you. Even when someone does something nice for you, you find yourself questioning their motives. You don't trust people, and you're afraid they will hurt you or let you down, so cynicism becomes your defense mechanism.

As we have seen, cynicism is toxic. It will rob you of all happiness. It can affect you in ways you would never expect—your job, your health, your relationships—and it will certainly hurt your relationship with God. As with all habits in life, recognizing the problem is always the first step to fixing it. Once you acknowledge your cynicism, you can then choose to respond differently. When you catch yourself being negative you can acknowledge your attitude and then take the following steps.

Steps to a Godly Habit

STEP 1: ACKNOWLEDGE THAT CYNICISM IS SIN

Once you acknowledge it's a problem in your life, then you must also recognize that it is not from God and therefore not a good thing. Paul said in Romans 14:23 that "everything that does not come from faith is sin" (NIV). While faith is complete trust or confidence in God, the very foundation of cynicism is our skepticism or unbelief.

People are often cynical because of the hurt and pain they have experienced, and in turn their cynicism causes them to spread hurt and pain to others. Just to be clear, the hurt and pain you feel is not sin. But when your response to hurt and pain is cynicism, that cynicism becomes sin. So confess it and ask God to forgive you for it. That is extremely hard for a cynic to do because, well, we are cynical. So to ask for forgiveness is to bring us back to trust in our God and give us a hope that he can work this out for our good. To ask for forgiveness humbles us, which helps to remove self-centered pride and dissolve anger.

STEP 2: BELIEVE THE BEST ABOUT PEOPLE

This will not happen unless you are intentional about it. Over time you have created a habit of always thinking the worst about people, so you have to create a new habit of thinking the best. Every time you get a negative thought about a situation or a person, stop right there and ask yourself what else it could mean. Try to find a more positive spin to put on the situation.

Maybe the girl at the checkout line in the grocery store isn't being friendly. Rather than jumping to the conclusion that she is a bad person, why not consider that maybe she is just having a bad day and you need to cut her some slack. Or maybe your husband is late for a dinner appointment. Instead of getting angry and immediately thinking he doesn't respect you, why not give him the benefit of the doubt. Maybe he got an unexpected call that made him late.

Scripture tells us that Satan is a liar who wants to give you negative thoughts about others, to bring division between you and the ones you love. He wants you to be cynical. In fact, Jesus told us in John 10:10, "The thief's purpose is to steal and kill and destroy." Satan will whisper those cynical lies into your ear: "That attorney did not represent your family well; all attorneys are bad." "Your parents' marriage failed because marriage doesn't work anymore." Satan wants to use the hurt you felt from one person to convince you everyone else will do the very same thing.

To counter Satan's lies we must focus on truth, and we must focus on the positive things about people and about God. That's why Paul tells us in Philippians 4:8, "And now, dear brothers and sisters, one final thing. Fix your thoughts on what is true, and honorable, and right, and pure, and lovely, and admirable. Think about things that are excellent and worthy of praise." We can choose what we think about, so decide today that you are going to focus on the things that are true and positive, and that you are always going to think the best about people. If you will be intentional to do that every day, you will replace cynicism with positive thoughts about others.

STEP 3: PRACTICE GRATITUDE

We have so much to be grateful for, but cynicism quickly clouds over all the good things in our life. And that's why it's important to practice expressing gratitude every day and in every situation.

A gratitude journal can really help. Every night before bed, try to write down two or three things you are grateful for. Then, with your journal in hand, start each day by thanking God for everything you have listed. I know this seems simple, but it can make a significant change in how you view things.

Then decide each day that you are going to thank several

people for how they have impacted your life, whether it be face-to-face or an e-mail or phone call.

Another thing I try to do is write five thank-you cards each week to people who have been a blessing in my life. The more you focus on the things you are grateful for, the more cynicism will fade. The more you focus on gratitude, the more it will remind you that God is the giver of all good gifts. James 1:17 says, "Whatever is good and perfect is a gift coming down to us from God our Father, who created all the lights in the heavens. He never changes or casts a shifting shadow." A heart of gratitude will leave no room for cynicism in your life.

STEP 4: PRACTICE FORGIVENESS AND COMPASSION

All throughout Scripture we are instructed in the importance of forgiving others just as Christ forgave us. We are also instructed in the importance of demonstrating compassion toward one another. For instance, Paul said in Ephesians 4:32, "Be kind and compassionate to one another, forgiving each other, just as in Christ God forgave you" (NIV). It's a fact that people are going to let you down; they are going to hurt your feelings. So then the question is, How will you respond to those hurts? If you are serious about fighting cynicism in your life, then you must forgive those who hurt you and demonstrate compassion toward them.

Several times over the years I've had people in my life who have annoyed me. I had to pray and ask God to forgive me for my negative feelings toward them and to help me love them. And I can honestly say that every single time God answered that prayer. When you cultivate compassion instead of resorting to cynicism, you will begin to feel closer to the people who are hard to love.

STEP 5: ENGAGE IN COMMUNITY

Isolation fuels cynicism. When you spend a lot of time alone, it's easy for your thoughts to go to places of self-pity or anger or even hopelessness. God never created us to be an island but to be in healthy relationships with others. Not to be dependent or independent but to be interdependent on one another. There is always a risk of getting hurt, but the benefits and spiritual health that will come from community far outweigh the risks. You will never become the person God has created you to be until you are plugged into healthy community.

STEP 6: SERVE ONE ANOTHER

Paul tells us in Ephesians 2:10 that "we are God's handiwork, created in Christ Jesus to do good works, which God prepared in advance for us to do" (NIV). The New Living Translation says, "We are God's masterpiece." In other words, you are God's handcrafted work of art, created to do good works. Cynicism thrives in a culture where people are bored, where people are not using their gifts and talents. So if you aren't already serving, find a place to start. Whether that's in your church or your community is not as important; what's important is that you do it.

Cynicism is a decision to stop trusting and believing. Is that really the way you want to live your life? Is that really the legacy you want people to remember you by? Cynics never change the world; they just tell you why the world can't change.

I love this excerpt from Carey Nieuwhof's book *Didn't See It Coming*:

> The cynics thought they were winning on the last Thursday of Jesus's life. They were certain they had the final word on Friday. They were in control. Despair had won. Even the disciples thought so. They went home, back to fishing. But nobody saw Sunday coming. Nobody saw hope rising. No one saw love breaking out from the ashes of hate. Nobody saw Jesus coming back.
>
> The remarkable part of Christianity is not that we have a Savior who came to deliver us but that we have a Savior who sees us for who we really are and loves us anyway. Jesus stared hate in the face and met it with love. He confronted despair and made it abundantly clear it wouldn't win.
>
> The thrust of the gospel is that Jesus sees *your* hate and meets it with love. He sees *your* despair and counters it with hope. He sees *your* doubt and lobs belief back at you again and again. Cynicism melts under the relentless hope of the gospel.[3]

I know life can be difficult at times. But don't let the cynical spirit of this age trick you into thinking there is nothing you can do about it. As believers we should be the most positive people on earth. Because we have this incredible assurance that God loves us and has a wonderful plan for our lives.

6

WORRY

Worry does not empty tomorrow of its sorrow, it empties today of its strength.

—Corrie ten Boom

When our daughter, Jenni, was pregnant with her fourth child, she and her husband, Andy, had three adorable daughters and were praying for a boy. I remember she even painted her toenails blue during her entire pregnancy. To our family's delight Griffin was born on the last day of January. In our mind he was perfect in every way. I loved holding and talking to this little guy.

When he was about a month old, I started to notice that he wasn't making eye contact. After a few months I finally said something about it to Jenni and Andy. They took Griffin to the doctor and he was diagnosed with ocular albinism, which means he doesn't have all the pigment in his eyes and his vision is only about 20–200.

That initial diagnosis was devastating. We didn't understand what this all meant for our precious little grandson. I found myself lying in bed every night worrying. Would he be able to ride a bike or play sports? Would he be able to drive a car? Would it limit his career?

And then the what-if questions would come. What if his eyesight gets worse? What if he doesn't recognize us? What if the other kids make fun of him? I prayed and kept saying I trusted God with Griffin's life, but the feelings of worry were relentless.

I know I am a pastor, and I am not supposed to worry. I am supposed to be the one who encourages others to trust God regardless of their circumstances. I can preach sermons, I can quote scripture, I can recite eloquent prayers in the brightness of the day, but when the darkness of the night settles in, I have to admit there are times I stare at the ceiling, feeling very much alone and full of worry. I understand what Proverbs 12:25 means when it says, "Worry weighs a person down."

But now that Griffin is in grade school, I realize it was foolish to have worried so much. Griffin still has the same problem with his eyes, but he is doing well in spite of it. He runs, he rides his bike, he rides his hoverboard, and he attends public school. He's just a typical kid excelling in all he does. My worrying about him didn't change anything. It didn't help him in any way whatsoever. It didn't encourage him at all. It was a total waste of time and emotional energy.

What about you? Are you a worrywart? A nervous Nellie? Does your anxiety keep you awake at night? Do you fret about anything and everything from your health to your kids' grades? Do you worry about job interviews, unpaid bills, rising gas prices, identity theft, or contagious diseases? (My newfound worry is book deadlines.)

Everybody thinks their worries are important, but let's be honest: some people fret over the silliest things.

"What am I going to do? Eight people saw me pick at my wedgie."

"I wonder how many people noticed this black speck in my teeth."

"Did anybody see me when I tripped over that chair and looked stupid?"

Worries, doubts, and anxieties have become a normal part of life. Over the span of a lifetime, worry can add up to endless hours of wasted time and emotional drain that you will never get back.

In this book, I'm discussing worry as it's defined by *Merriam-Webster*: "mental distress or agitation resulting from concern usually for something impending or anticipated."[1] Someone once said, "Worry is faith in the negative, trust in the unpleasant, assurance of disaster and belief in defeat . . . worry is wasting today's time to clutter up tomorrow's opportunities with yesterday's troubles."[2]

It's important to note that there are times when the line between worry and clinical anxiety can become blurred. If you're finding it difficult to manage on your own, I encourage you to seek the help of a trained mental health professional.

Worry is not a good thing—unless maybe it happens to be one of these situations:

- you see a *60 Minutes* news team waiting in your office
- the horn on your car goes off accidentally and remains stuck as you follow a group of Hells Angels on the highway

- the bird singing outside your window is a buzzard
- you wake up and your braces are locked together
- you call your answering service and they tell you it's none of your business
- your income tax check bounces
- your wife says, "Good morning, Bill," but your name is George

Now a lot of people think worry and fear are cut from the same mold, but they are not exactly the same thing. Fear is what you might feel when you are flying in an airplane and hear the plane is having mechanical problems.

Worry, on the other hand, is the anticipation of some experience. You keep asking what-if questions and manufacturing answers you don't like. For instance, maybe every time you board an airplane you start to worry the plane might go down, even though the probability of that happening is very low. But while you are worrying, you are missing out on the world going on all around you. Erma Bombeck is credited with saying, "Worry is like a rocking chair: it gives you something to do but never gets you anywhere."[3] Simply put, worry doesn't work; it's stewing without doing. It's like revving the engine of a car while it's in neutral. It might use a lot of energy, but you are not getting anywhere.

I have heard it said that the ignorant worry because they don't know enough. The knowledgeable worry because they know too much. The rich worry because they are afraid of losing what they have. The poor worry because they don't have enough. The old worry because they are facing death. The young worry because they are facing life.

I also read that 40 percent of the things we worry about will never happen. Thirty percent of the things we worry about are over and can't be changed. Twelve percent of our worries are needless ones about our health. Ten percent of our time worrying is spent on petty, miscellaneous concerns. Only 8 percent of the things we worry about are legitimate concerns that we can do something about.[4]

So that means that 92 percent of our worries are unnecessary!

The sixth chapter of Matthew is a part of Jesus' famous Sermon on the Mount. In this sermon Jesus showed people how following him was going to differ from following the Old Testament Law. In fact, seven times in the chapter Jesus said, "Don't worry." Here's an example:

> That is why I tell you not to worry about everyday life—whether you have enough food and drink, or enough clothes to wear. Isn't life more than food, and your body more than clothing? Look at the birds. They don't plant or harvest or store food in barns, for your heavenly Father feeds them. And aren't you far more valuable to him than they are? Can all your worries add a single moment to your life?
>
> (MATT. 6:25–27)

When Jesus commands his disciples not to worry about earthly things, such as food and clothing, that doesn't mean he wants us to walk around starving and naked. It just means that instead of being distracted and preoccupied by material things, we need to focus on the things of God. Jesus is reminding us that God has promised to supply our material needs.

If I told my kids that from now on I would make their car payments, do you think they would ever worry about those car payments again? Of course not. They would no longer give it a thought because they know me, and they know I will keep my word. If that is true with me, how much more is it true with our heavenly Father?

To worry about something you can't change is useless, and to worry about something you can change, well . . . it's kind of dumb. If you can change it, then change it. Don't sit and worry about it.

Jesus also gave us an analogy using birds. Now I admit I don't know a lot about birds, but I don't think they do all that much. It's not like the survival of mankind depends on a few birds getting enough to eat. And yet God feeds them. He said, "If I take care of the birds of the air, don't you think you are a lot more important to me than they are?" A few verses later he gave another example about flowers. Have you ever looked at the beauty of a flower, the detail that God put into making something that won't last but a few weeks? This was his point: Animals don't worry. Plants don't worry. The only thing in all creation that worries is people.

Have you ever heard it said that worry just comes naturally for someone? Well, actually it doesn't. Worry is a learned behavior. We might learn it from a family member, such as a parent or grandparent, we might learn it from other children in our lives, or we could even learn it from watching television.

While we all worry from time to time, it can take a toll on your health if it sticks around long enough. Something as small as a nagging concern in the back of your mind can affect your heart. It can make you more likely to have high blood pressure, a heart attack, or a stroke.[5]

Dr. Charles Mayo of the Mayo Clinic said, "Worry affects circulation, the heart, the glands, the whole nervous system, and profoundly affects the heart. I have never known a man who died from overwork, but many who died from doubt."[6]

The Mayo Clinic actually estimates that more than 80 percent of their total caseload is directly related to worry on the part of their patients and noted that "52 percent of the people in the hospital could get up and leave if they could rid themselves of fear, worry and frustration."[7] Two meta-analytic studies conducted in 2000 found that the average child of the 1980s exhibited more anxiety than child *psychiatric patients* of the 1950s.[8]

I once heard a story about a woman who, for forty years, every time she got a cramp was convinced it was the beginning of stomach cancer. And yet when she was seventy-three, she died of pneumonia. She wasted forty years of her life worrying about the wrong disease!

We're often like a patient in the psychiatric hospital, holding his ear close to the wall, listening intently. The nurse finally approaches and says, "What are you doing?" The patient says, "Shhh," and continues listening. Finally, the patient motions for the nurse to come over and listen. She puts her ear to the wall for a long time and then finally says, "I can't hear a thing." The patient says, "I know. It's been like that all day!"

Worry is a good indication that you have a misunderstanding of the heart of God. You feel like he's not going to be there for you, and yet Paul wrote in Philippians 4:19, "And this same God who takes care of me will supply all your needs from his glorious riches, which have been given to us in Christ Jesus."

Isn't it strange how we are willing to believe God to forgive our sins and save our soul, but when it comes to any other area of our life, we find it hard to trust him? "I will trust God with my eternity, but I am worried about my finances." "I will trust him with my eternity, but I am worried about my marriage." Do you see how absurd that is? If you can trust God to forgive your sins and give you the promise of eternal life, don't you think you can trust him with every other area of your life?

Henri Nouwen gave an example of a lesson he learned about trust from a family of trapeze artists known as the Flying Rodleighs. He asked one of the acrobats how he knew that guy on the other side would catch him.

> The secret . . . is that the flyer does nothing and the catcher does everything. When I fly to Joe [my catcher], I have simply to stretch out my arms and hands and wait for him to catch me and pull me safely over the apron behind the catchbar. . . .
>
> The worst thing the flyer can do is to try to catch the catcher. I am not supposed to catch Joe. It's Joe's task to catch me. If I grabbed Joe's wrists, I might break them, or he might break mine, and that would be the end for both of us. A flyer must fly, and a catcher must catch, and the flyer must trust, with outstretched arms, that his catcher will be there for him.[9]

You don't need to worry. God will catch you.

You might believe that worrying is the responsible thing to do, that it helps you avoid bad things or prepares you for the worst. Or maybe you tell yourself that if you worry about a problem long enough, you will eventually figure out the solution. Or maybe you believe if you worry about something it demonstrates to others that you care about it. But that's actually not true. Worry doesn't show care for someone. It shows only a lack of trust in God. And it is possible to care about something or someone without worrying. Once you understand that worrying is the problem and not the solution, you can begin to break the habit in your life.

You can't read the Bible without getting the message that worry is sin. For instance, Hebrews 11:6 says, "It is impossible to please God without faith." In Philippians 4:6 Paul said, "Do not be anxious about anything" (NIV). I would again tell you that while fear can be a good thing in your life, worry never is.

Worry is a mental habit that can be broken. With God's help you can train your brain to stay calm and look at life from a less fearful perspective.

Now before I give you some helpful steps to overcome the habit of worry in your life, I want you to write down what you think your greatest worry in life is right now. What is keeping you awake at night? ______________

Own It

Now while it's true that we all worry at times, don't be fooled into thinking that your worry is helpful. Some people have convinced themselves that worry is actually a part of the process of solving a problem; it is not. There is absolutely nothing worry can do to help alleviate problems.

Worry will affect your outlook on life in a negative way, and it will make you feel like you are always under a dark cloud. I heard one guy describe it as experiencing low-grade depression all the time. It will also have a detrimental effect on your productivity at work and even your social life. You will find it hard to have healthy relationships because your attention will always be on your worries. And it can't help but affect your relationship with God in a negative way. To worry says, "I don't trust you to take care of this problem, God, so I am going to hold on to it."

The first thing you need to do is to acknowledge that worry has become a problem for you. The most dangerous emotions are often the ones you deny. You cannot begin to break a habit if you don't admit it's a problem. Once you've called it out, you are then ready to take the necessary steps to break the habit of worry.

Steps to a Godly Habit

STEP 1: MAKE SURE GOD IS THE CENTER OF YOUR LIFE

Just as you have learned to worry, you can also learn to trust God. Jesus said, "Seek the Kingdom of God above all else, and live righteously, and he will give you everything you need" (Matt. 6:33). I need to remind you that worry is an indication of mixed values. Whenever you start worrying it means that something that is dear to you is being held outside of your faith in Christ.

Jesus should be the source of your spiritual life. If you want to experience peace of mind, then he must be the Lord of everything you care about. For instance, if you haven't included Christ in your finances, then finances will become a source of worry for you. If you haven't included him in the raising of your kids, then your kids will be a source of worry for you. Any area of your life that God is not the Lord of will eventually become a source of worry for you.

STEP 2: IDENTIFY YOUR WORRIES

Yes, I mean actually make a worry list. Throughout the day if you notice you are worried about something, write it down. Come back to your list once a day with the intent of lifting those things up to God in prayer. Then remind yourself there is no need to worry. God's got this; you can trust him.

STEP 3: CULTIVATE FAITH

I heard about a man who would race his two horses and take bets on which horse would win. He always seemed to know which horse would win each day. Someone asked the man how he always seemed to know. He said, "It's easy. The horse I feed will always win." Feed your faith and you will starve worry!

When you allow worry to come in the front door of your heart, faith is sliding out the back. The presence of worry means the absence of faith. Therefore, if you don't want to worry then you must cultivate faith. The more your faith grows the less room there is for worry.

When I was in grade school several of the kids in the neighborhood walked to and from school each day. The shortest route was down a street where a man had a large dog, a boxer. It had a very intimidating bark and was tethered to a long chain in the backyard. When we would walk past this house that dog would start barking and come running after us. Of course, the chain would eventually stop him, but we were always worried that one day he would break loose and attack us. I would start worrying about that dog blocks before I ever reached the house.

One day the owner of the dog was in the backyard and watched this entire scene unfold. The next day, as we walked by the house, the man was once again outside, only this time he had the dog on a leash. When he saw us, he began to motion for us to come over to him. We didn't know if we were in trouble or if he was going to let his dog bite us, but either way we were not walking over to him.

Then he started walking over to us. The entire time the man kept saying to us, "You don't need to be afraid of my dog." Then he knelt down and pulled back the dog's upper lip to reveal he had no teeth! Seriously there was not a tooth in that dog's mouth. The man said, "Even if this dog were to ever get loose and try to bite you, it wouldn't hurt." All of us started to laugh. And we were never afraid of that dog again. When that man told us the truth, all of the fears and worries we had about that dog were instantly gone.

The most common tool in Satan's toolbox is to lie to us. In talking about the devil, Jesus said, "He has always hated the truth, because there is no truth in him. When he lies, it is consistent with his character; for he is a liar and the father of lies" (John 8:44).

Because Satan is a spirit, he can whisper lies into our spirit. If we believe those lies to be true, we will respond accordingly. He wants to bring worry and fear on you by whispering into your ear a whole lot of what-ifs about things that may not even be true. But what you will find is, like that dog, the devil has no teeth, and his bark is worse than his bite.

On the other hand, when we learn truth, our faith, or trust in God, is cultivated. Romans 10:17 says, "faith comes by hearing, and hearing by the word of God" (NKJV). The Bible says that faith is a result of hearing, trusting, and believing the truth of God's Word.

The best way to cultivate your faith is to study the Word of God on a regular basis. Jesus said, "If you hold to my teaching, you are really my disciples. Then you will know the truth, and the truth will set you free" (John 8:31–32 NIV). It is the Word of God that wakens our faith and dispels our greatest fears and worries.

STEP 4: PRAY

Prayer refocuses our attention away from our worries and back onto Christ. Which might just be why Paul said in 1 Thessalonians 5:17 to "never stop praying." When you worry, you are not praying. But when you pray, you are not worrying.

Paul instructs us in Philippians 4:6–7, "Don't worry about anything; instead, pray about everything. Tell God what you need, and thank him for all he has done. Then you will experience God's peace, which exceeds anything we can understand. His peace will guard your hearts and minds as you live in Christ Jesus." Paul made it clear we are not to worry, and the remedy is to pray. And the more we pray, the more we will experience the peace of God.

If you don't think your situation is worth praying about, then it's certainly not worth worrying about. But if you have something that's causing you to worry, turn it over to God.

STEP 5: LIVE ONE DAY AT A TIME

When Jesus was teaching his disciples how to pray, part of his prayer was, "Give us *today* the food we need" (Matt. 6:11, emphasis mine). He didn't say to pray for your month's allotment of food. He wanted them to depend on him and trust him one day at a time.

A few verses later Jesus instructed his disciples, "So don't worry about tomorrow, for tomorrow will bring its own worries. Today's trouble is enough for today" (v. 34).

In other words, don't open your umbrella until it starts to rain. You know there are two days of the week you should never worry about—yesterday and tomorrow. Because when you fret over yesterday's problems and then worry about what might happen tomorrow, you miss out on the blessings of today. As Charles Spurgeon wrote over a hundred years ago:

> Enough for today is all we can enjoy. We cannot eat or drink or wear more than today's supply of food and clothing. The surplus gives us the care of storing it and the anxiety that someone might steal it. One staff aids a traveler; a bunch of staves is a heavy burden. Enough is as good as a feast and more than gluttony can enjoy. Enough is all we should expect, a craving for more is ungratefulness. When our Father doesn't give you more, be content with your daily allowance.[10]

Stop focusing on your worries so you can focus on all that is already good in your world.

STEP 6: BE A PROBLEM SOLVER

Once you have finished the first five steps, it's time to put on your problem-solver hat. Choose a time when you are most relaxed, but not right before you go to bed, to sit down with your worry list and figure out solutions. Decide what action steps you are going to take today for each item on your list.

For example, if you are worried about your bills, then maybe your first action step today is to call your creditors to see if they will work out a payment plan. If a friend has just gotten home from the hospital, maybe today you fix them a meal or cut their grass.

Many of the worries on your list will be beyond your ability to fix or even do anything about. That's when you do what the scripture encourages us to do, "Give all your worries and cares to God, for he cares about you" (1 Peter 5:7).

Don't get discouraged; you have everything you need to stop worrying. Just use these steps and practice them on a daily basis. You can release your worries and experience God's peace.

Did you know there are more than seven thousand promises in God's Word? I think that is enough to cover any struggle you might have. If God loves you enough to send his own Son to die for you, don't you think he loves you enough to care for every other need you might have? God has seen to it that you will never face a negative situation without a promise powerful enough to help you through it.

Do you worry that God has given up on you? He said in Hebrews 13:5, "I will never leave you nor forsake you" (NKJV).

Do you worry about dying? Jesus declared, "I am the resurrection and the life. He who believes in Me, though he may die, he shall live" (John 11:25 NKJV).

Do you feel weak? "He gives strength to those who are tired and more power to those who are weak" (Isa. 40:29 NCV).

Regardless of what you are worried about, there is a promise in the Bible to help you work through it. So why not start today by giving God that one area of worry you wrote down earlier? Release the regrets from yesterday, refuse the fears of tomorrow, and receive the peace he has for you today.

7

COMPLAINING

> If you have time to whine and complain
> about something, then you have the
> time to do something about it.
>
> —Anthony J. D'Angelo

Winters can get really cold and gray in Indiana, so every February Sandy and I go to beautiful, sunny Florida. One afternoon we were sitting out by the pool, reading while enjoying a cold drink. A man walked by us, looking for a place to sit. There were a couple of chairs next to me, so I decided to be friendly and make small talk. I said, "Man, can you believe how hot it is today? The humidity level is through the roof!"

He responded, "I don't know . . . It's certainly better than the deep freeze the folks in the Midwest are experiencing right now." He then turned and walked away.

I said to Sandy, "What's his problem? I was just trying to be friendly!"

I was doing what I had done so many times before, using complaining as a way to connect with someone, almost like an ice-breaker or a way to find common ground. I mean, nothing unites people quite like a common dislike or frustration, right? And yet complaining is a poor way to connect with people.

But most of us are like the rest of us—we do it anyway. We nag and whine, we groan and criticize, we mumble and complain with alarming regularity.

"I get so tired of all the traffic."

"Why do gas prices have to be so high?"

"I hate it when people cut in line."

No one likes to be around that person who feels the need to vocalize every disappointment in life, who seems to have the ability to find the dark cloud in every silver lining. In reality he may do it so much he doesn't even realize it's become a habit. While you might think he is the most negative person to be around, he has convinced himself that the world is negative, and he is just properly responding to an annoying situation.

Guy Winch at *Psychology Today* explains the difference:

> Optimists see: *A glass half full.*
>
> Pessimists see: *A glass half empty.*
>
> Chronic complainers see: *A glass that is slightly chipped holding water that isn't cold enough, probably because it's tap water even though I asked for bottled, and wait, there's a smudge on the rim, too, which means the glass wasn't cleaned properly and now I'll probably end up with some kind of virus. Why do these things always happen to me?*[1]

Complainers are unaware of how they are negatively affecting others. I like this quote by former major league baseball player Paul Molitor: "Complaining is like vomiting. You might feel better after you get it out, but you make everybody around you sick."[2]

As a child how many times did you hear, "Stop grumbling," "Stop whining," and "Do what you are told"? Complaining is the grown-up version of whining.

As followers of Christ we are supposed to model our lives after his example. Can you imagine the Son of God ever complaining?

"Man, why do I have to die on the cross for all these sins when I've done nothing wrong?"

"This headache from that crown of thorns is killing me."

"This cross is so heavy. Why do I have to carry it so far?"

"I shouldn't have to wake up from my nap to calm a storm. They don't trust me. I'm going back to bed."

And yet complaining is something most Christians become prone to. If it's your own actions that caused a situation, you have no reason to complain. And if you complain, do it to the right person—your friends don't want to hear about it. Rather than gossiping, go directly to someone and resolve an issue. It's all about how you handle it. The point is, you don't have to constantly complain about every little thing that isn't the way you like it. Seriously, what non-Christian would be attracted to the Christian lifestyle if all they hear is us complaining?

A. W. Tozer once said, "Among those sins most exquisitely fitted to injure the soul and destroy the testimony, few can equal the sin of complaining."[3]

So whether it's whining or complaining, it's all the same thing. What you will find is that complainers come in all ages, genders, and nationalities. There is even a phrase to describe complaining: to "vent one's spleen," which is to express or air your feelings of frustration or anger. In other words, "Bill often vents his spleen at his wife whenever things are not good at the office." Eckhart Tolle once said, "When you complain, you make yourself into a victim. . . . Leave the situation or accept it. All else is madness."[4]

Speaking of madness, I read about a man who robbed a Wendy's fast-food restaurant. He was so mad about the amount of loot that he later called the store to complain—not once but *twice*. In the first call he said, "Next time there better be more than $586."[5]

Then I read about a man named Arthur Bundrage, who robbed a bank. He was arrested after he returned to the bank to complain about the bank's service. He had demanded twenty thousand from the cashier but later discovered she had not given him the full amount.[6]

And then we often complain about what are called first-world problems. These are problems that come from living in a wealthy, industrialized nation. Problems that would cause people living in third-world countries to roll their eyes or shake their heads in disbelief.

For instance, you might complain, "The neighbor's dog pooped on my well-manicured lawn." Or, "My daddy bought me a *used* car today. I'm disappointed. I thought I was getting a *new* car." Or, "My electric toothbrush just broke and now I have to move my arm back and forth to brush my teeth!" Or, "It is so frustrating; we have three cars at our house but only a two-car garage." This type of complaining is rooted in our inability to realize how good we really have it.

Author Will Bowen said, "Complaining is an epidemic that is destroying our happiness, relationships, health, and success. The problem is that most people aren't even aware when they complain. . . . Complaining is like bad breath—you notice it when it comes out of someone else's mouth, but not when it [comes] out of your own."[7]

We find ourselves complaining about anything and everything, so much that it becomes part of our daily lives. And yet nobody wants to be "that person," you know, "the complainer."

Complaining can also be contagious. You get one disgruntled complainer, and it won't be long before it spreads to someone close by. I certainly see it happen in my home. When I'm complaining it's easy for Sandy to add her thoughts or her own frustrations to what I'm whining about.

Some healthy, solution-oriented venting with your spouse or with a close friend can prove to be constructive and cathartic, as well as foster a deeper connection between the two of you. For instance, when you get home at the end of your day, it can be helpful to vent if there's a problem at work, as long as you are venting about the problem and not finding fault with a person. It's the idea of trust and emotional support, to know that your spouse or even a friend will be there for you. However, if you cannot bring it around to a solution or to how God might use this in your life, then complaining will end up having a negative effect on your relationship.

I used to think people complained because they had a lot of frustrations, but I now believe that people create a lot of their frustrations because they complain. Complainers are "missionaries of misery." It takes no special skill, talent, or IQ. Any idiot can do it, and not only does it hurt you, but it hurts those around you.

I like the story of the man who decided to join a monastery and one of the rules of this particular monastic group was that you were only allowed to speak two words at the end of every ten years. At the end of his first ten years he said, "Food bad!" At the end of his second ten years, he said, "Bed hard!" Finally, on his thirtieth anniversary at the monastery, he said, "I quit!" The monk in charge responded, "It doesn't surprise me one bit. You've done nothing but complain ever since you got here."

While complaining is part of our culture, it certainly didn't start with us; it actually goes all the way back to Adam and Eve. Adam was the first complainer. He did what he wasn't supposed to do when he ate of the forbidden fruit, blaming his wife and complaining to God about it: "It was the woman you gave me who gave me the fruit, and I ate it" (Gen. 3:12).

If there has ever been a group that was known for complaining, it was the Israelites of the Old Testament. Even after God delivered them from 430 years of slavery in Egypt by parting the waters of the Red Sea, they still complained against him. Exodus 16:3 says, "'If only the Lord had killed us back in Egypt,' they moaned. 'There we sat around pots filled with meat and ate all the bread we wanted. But now you have brought us into this wilderness to starve us all to death.'"

The complaining didn't stop there. They complained about their food, they complained about all they felt they had left behind in Egypt, and they complained about their leaders. "Now when the people complained, it displeased the Lord; for the Lord heard it, and His anger was aroused" (Num. 11:1 NKJV).

Another time Moses was whining to God about how the people complained all the time. Essentially, God said, "They may be complaining to you, but they are actually complaining about me." The same is true with us today. To murmur, or complain, is a failure to trust God's plan or a failure to like God's plan; either way it is a sin against God because you are being ungrateful for all that he has given you.

The Israelites demonstrated such a lack of faith by their constant complaining until God finally had enough and said that except for Joshua and Caleb, none of that generation would ever see the promised land. In the same way, the unbelief or lack of faith demonstrated through your complaining will only keep you from God's best in your life.

And yet please understand that complaining doesn't make you a bad person. It can just keep you from being the kind of person Christ wants you to be. It's a denial of responsibility, and blame is just another way of excusing yourself from being responsible.

Let me show you why complaining offends the heart of God. Imagine you are a parent trying to do a lot for your kids, but all they do is whine and complain about how unfair you are or how bad they have it. As a parent, you just want to lovingly say, "Sweetheart, you are so ungrateful!" Well, I can't help but wonder if God ever feels the same way when all we do is complain. If you want to hurt the heart of God, or if you want to drive people away, just keep on complaining. On the other hand, if you want your life to honor God, then you've got to stop it.

As I mentioned earlier, it's like complainers have spiritual bad breath! When you talk to someone with bad breath, what do you do? You take a step back, don't you? The same thing happens when you complain—people want to take a step back from you.

It reminds me of a story about the great English preacher John Wesley back in the 1700s. One Sunday morning after his sermon, a lady walked up to him and said, "Brother Wesley, are you open to some criticism?"

He said, "I guess so. What would you like to criticize?"

She said, "The ribbons on your tie are entirely too long and inappropriate for a man of God." The woman then took out a pair of scissors and cut off his tie!

People standing nearby were shocked, but then Wesley calmly asked her, "May I borrow the scissors for a moment?"

She handed him the scissors and he said, "Ma'am, are you open to some criticism?"

She said, "Well, I suppose so."

Wesley said, "Good, would you please stick out your tongue?"[8]

Some might think that by complaining you are merely observing what's going on. But complaining, like all thought patterns, is not mere observation; it's a creative act. When you complain, you are simply reinforcing negative thoughts, and the more you complain, the more you summon your creative energies to encourage the very thing you complain about. It has been said that when you complain, you are really placing your order for more of the same. At the very least you're dwelling on the negative and definitely reinforcing what you don't want.

I read recently that most people complain thirty times a day. But, of course, there are some who never complain. Dr. Laura Marham wrote, "Their lives, from the outside, aren't any different from anyone else's. They didn't win the lottery. But they rate themselves as happier than other people. Their relationships are closer. They live longer. And while I haven't yet seen any research on this, I'd bet they're happier parents."[9]

Own It

Have you ever noticed how two people can go through the same experience and yet have opposite responses? One person sees the positive benefits while the other person has nothing but complaints. It's because complainers aren't looking for the upside; they are looking for sympathy.

We all complain at times, and things are never quite as good as we want them to be. But for some folks, complaining becomes such a habit we don't even notice we are doing it anymore. Constantly vocalizing your negative thoughts is not a good thing for many reasons. Useless complaining makes things seem worse than what they actually are. And it can certainly be draining and annoying to our friends and family.

Are you complaining a lot? Listen carefully to yourself at home and at work; is your first response usually a negative one? Are your responses reflecting a negative image of you to others? If so, then you need to recognize it as a habit in your life so that you can begin to deal with it in a productive way.

As I said, complaining can be annoying to others, especially when the complainer seems unwilling to do anything to resolve the issues or rejects help and advice on how to solve the problem. Once you realize it's a problem, then you can take the necessary steps to break this habit.

Steps to a Godly Habit

STEP 1: UNDERGO A COMPLAINT DETOX

Frequent complaining can lead to poor health and employment issues, and as you might imagine, it can destroy healthy relationships too. So you need to take steps to stop this habit in your life.

Author Will Bowen came up with the idea of a Complaint

Detox. He founded a movement called A Complaint Free World and "has spent years urging people to give up moaning about their lives" for twenty-one days. His idea was to wear a bracelet on your wrist as a visual reminder that you're trying to rid yourself of all complaining. If you do complain, you must move the bracelet to the other wrist and start again. The idea is to try and go for twenty-one days without ever allowing a complaint to pass over your lips. In the first few days you will most likely be moving the bracelet a lot. But over a few weeks it should slow down as you become more aware of the complaining.[10]

"Do everything without complaining and arguing, so that no one can criticize you. Live clean, innocent lives as children of God, shining like bright lights in a world full of crooked and perverse people" (Phil. 2:14–15).

STEP 2: PRACTICE BEING POSITIVE

Like many people, I have a love-hate relationship with complaining. There is something very satisfying about letting someone know just how unhappy I am about something. On the other hand, I don't want to be that guy who whines all the time. I want to be known for being a positive person.

But there are times I let my guard down for various reasons. Maybe I hurt physically or I just don't feel good and I have allowed it to affect my attitude. Or maybe I've had an argument with my wife or there is a conflict at work and it is affecting me emotionally. Fear, anger, and pain can all affect me in a negative way. Which is why I need to be aware of those things going on in my life and intentionally look for something positive to say about every situation.

For instance, let's say you planned to go for a bike ride this

Saturday, but you get rained out. What is something positive that can come out of that?

Well, besides the fact you may need the rain, you could stay home and relax with a good book in front of a window while enjoying the rain. There are always two choices you can move toward. Decide you are going to choose the one with the positive outcome.

Sometimes you think it will make you feel better if you can complain and get it off your chest. But you would be wrong, according to Robin Kowalski, PhD, author of *Complaining, Teasing, and Other Annoying Behaviors*. She said that complaining without a real purpose won't lead to happiness. When we vent just to vent, it's destructive. Instead of verbalizing it, her advice is to write it down as a way to express it. And then to simply throw it away.[11]

I would encourage you to start your day with something that sets your attitude in a positive frame of mind. Maybe that's listening to worship music or reading Scripture or memorizing Scripture or listening to a sermon. Whatever it might be, find something that will focus your attitude on the things of God. Paul said, "Fix your thoughts on what is true, and honorable, and right, and pure, and lovely, and admirable. Think about things that are excellent and worthy of praise" (Phil. 4:8).

STEP 3: PRACTICE EXPRESSING GRATITUDE

When you complain, you focus on what's wrong, but when you express gratitude, you focus on the positive blessings in your life. Colossians 4:2 says we are to be devoted to giving thanks, and Psalm 116:17 says we are to make our lives a thanksgiving offering before the Lord.

Michael Zigarelli, the author of *Cultivating Christian Character*, talks about a study he did of more than five thousand believers worldwide. For the study he compared a group of what he called "high-virtue Christians" (people who consistently displayed the fruit of the Spirit) to a group of what he called "average-virtue Christians." He wanted to see what made the high-virtue Christians different. The one characteristic that clearly stood out above all the rest was gratitude.[12]

Zigarelli quoted philosopher Marcus Tullius Cicero, who argued that gratitude is not only the greatest of virtues but "the parent of all the others." Zigarelli went on to say, "Call it whatever you'd like. . . . Gratitude is a powerful disposition that provides us with a very efficient, very effective mechanism for developing myriad character traits. Want more inner peace? Work on gratitude. Want more patience? Work on gratitude. Want to be more compassionate? You get the idea."[13]

I believe the most important step in developing inner peace is to quit complaining and start demonstrating thanksgiving and gratitude to God. Jesus said, "A good man brings good things out of the good stored up in his heart, and an evil man brings evil things out of the evil stored up in his heart. For the mouth speaks what the heart is full of" (Luke 6:45 NIV). If your heart is not right with God, then it's hard to stop complaining.

A right relationship with God has nothing to do with our circumstances but everything to do with our heart. In other words, you can be going through a difficult time, but you refuse to whine and complain about it because you know that God loves you and has promised to work things together for your good.

Paul is a great example of someone who lived that out. He wrote his letter to the Philippians from a prison cell. I'm sure in his mind this looked like the end of the road. He knew he was probably going to die there, but look at what he said: "But I will rejoice even if I lose my life" (Phil. 2:17). Most people would be complaining, "I don't like being in prison. I didn't do anything wrong. This isn't fair. I've been falsely accused." Instead he chose to express gratitude to God.

How can a guy in a prison cell have that attitude? I can tell you how. This is the same guy who also wrote, "My old self has been crucified with Christ. It is no longer I who live, but Christ lives in me. So I live in this earthly body by trusting in the Son of God, who loved me and gave himself for me" (Gal. 2:20). Paul knew that he had been forgiven and transformed into the image of Christ. You could almost hear him say, "If you knew where I came from, if you knew what I've been forgiven of, you would understand why I trust him completely. You would know why I have no reason to complain: God has a plan for my life, and I trust him."

I would encourage you to keep a journal and every day write down at least five things that you are thankful for. It will refocus you on the blessings in your life. I know you might argue, "But how am I supposed to be thankful when I just lost my job or when I can't pay my bills?" It's not that you are thankful *for* your circumstance, but you are thankful *in* your circumstance. It's the attitude that says, "God, I don't like this situation I find myself in, and I don't understand it, but I am grateful that you have a plan, and you have promised to work it out for my good."

Paul wrote, "Rejoice in the Lord always. I will say it again: Rejoice!" (Phil. 4:4 NIV). From a prison cell, Paul made a personal choice to be grateful to God regardless of his circumstances. If you want to get rid of the complaining in your life, you need to make that same choice.

STEP 4: PRACTICE BEING CONTENT

Life throws a lot of curveballs our way. And those curveballs can often create a great deal of discontent. My wife and I wanted to build a new home, but we knew financially we needed to wait about a year. However, since there were two lots we had our eyes on, we decided to go ahead and purchase the lot and then wait a year to build. We contacted a real estate agent who said the lots were selling very quickly. We really liked both lots and had a hard time deciding which lot we preferred. But by the time we made a decision and called the agent back, we discovered that both lots had been sold.

We were so disappointed, and for weeks I was grumbling and complaining to anyone who would listen. I was mad at the agent, I was mad at myself—I was even mad at God! *Why would God allow this to happen?* I thought. I could already picture our house sitting on that lot. We had spent a lot of time on the phone with the real estate agent and the builder; this was supposed to be *our* lot. There weren't any more lots available in the area we wanted.

This complaining went on for several weeks until my wife finally said, "Steve, you need to let this go." I then began to realize how foolish I was being. One of my favorite verses in Scripture has always been Jeremiah 29:11: "'For I know the plans I have for you,' says the Lord. 'They are plans for good and not for disaster, to give you a future and a hope.'" I knew that God loved me and if he closed the door on us getting that lot then it just wasn't supposed to be. I asked God to forgive me for my attitude and put it all back in his hands. We decided we would shelve the idea and look again in a year.

A year later I noticed the lot we originally wanted was still empty. I stopped and asked the guy living next door to the lot if he knew what the new owners were going to do. He said he wasn't sure, but he gave me the new owner's name and phone number. I contacted them and told them I was interested in the lot. They said they had not been able to sell their home and would be glad to sell us the lot for the same price they paid for it.

So we ended up getting the same lot a year later, which was when we were actually ready to build. Once again, I was reminded that I just need to trust God. The apostle Paul wrote, "I know how to live on almost nothing or with everything. I have learned the secret of living in every situation, whether it is with a full stomach or empty, with plenty or little. For I can do everything through Christ, who gives me strength" (Phil. 4:12–13).

Not everything in life is going to be good, but I can be content because I know that God is going to somehow work it out for my good if I will just trust him. Romans 8:28 says it well, "And we know that in all things God works for the good of those who love him, who have been called according to his purpose" (NIV). Another great verse is, "But godliness with contentment is great gain" (1 Tim. 6:6 NIV). It might also help to repeat the serenity prayer: "God grant me the serenity to accept the things I cannot change, the courage to change the things I can, and the wisdom to know the difference."

STEP 5: BE LESS JUDGMENTAL

Early in our adult life, Sandy and I became friends with a couple from our church. The pastor of our church was new and creating a lot of problems in the church. It was common for us to sit around with our newfound friends and complain about what a terrible job we thought he was doing. We were building our friendship around complaining. And as hard as it is to admit, I looked forward to these weekly complaint fests.

The truth is there were serious problems going on with this pastor, and there are times when it is entirely appropriate to raise attention to a wrong being committed. But what we were doing was not helping. We were finding fault without making any effort to make things better. We didn't show this man the courtesy to even talk with him about it. Rather than simply complaining, the Bible makes it clear that we have a responsibility to go to the person. "If another believer sins against you, go privately and point out the offense. If the other person listens and confesses it, you have won that person back. But if you are unsuccessful, take one or two others with you and go back again, so that everything you say may be confirmed by two or three witnesses" (Matt. 18:15–16). Jesus also said, "Do not judge, or you too will be judged" (Matt. 7:1 NIV).

STEP 6: BITE YOUR TONGUE

In grade school I had a teacher who used to say, "If you can't say anything good about someone, just don't say anything at all." I am sure you have complained about things that you were later sorry for. Sometimes the wisest thing you can do is bite your tongue.

That's what Isaiah said about the coming Messiah. "He was oppressed and treated harshly, yet he never said a word. He was led like a lamb to the slaughter. And as a sheep is silent before the shearers, he did not open his mouth" (Isa. 53:7). In Isaiah 52:14 it tells us his face was so disfigured he hardly seemed human. He was then hung on a cross, naked, to die for you and for me, and yet there was not a word of complaint. The next time someone does something that annoys you, remember what Jesus did for us and bite your tongue.

There may be times it is necessary to complain. When you do, just make sure to keep your emotions in check and do it with the intent to solve the problem. Make sure you complain only to the person who can actually fix the problem, and then always try to end on a positive note.

I am not saying it will be easy, but if you will take these steps, you can break the habit of complaining and start a new habit of expressing gratitude to the Lord for all he has done in your life.

8

WORKAHOLISM

For workaholics, all the eggs of self-esteem are in the basket of work.

—Judith M. Bardwick

"Hi, my name is Steve, and I'm a workaholic."

If you have ever been to a recovery group or seen one on television, you recognize that opening sentence. If there's an addiction I've ever struggled with, it's workaholism. If not an addiction, it's certainly been a bad habit in my life.

I love to work, and a big part of it is that I love what I do. For me it's more than a job; it's what I believe God has called me to do. And when I'm doing it, I feel God's pleasure. And yet, I should not use my calling as an excuse to justify my need to overwork. And if I'm being honest, I've struggled with this issue long before I was ever in ministry.

The term *workaholism* was first introduced in 1971 by minister and psychologist Wayne Oates to describe the uncontrollable need to work. It was compared to alcoholism, due to the similar destructive compulsion that characterizes both conditions.[1]

So, in that sense, you could say I took my first drink of achievement when I was twenty-one years old and opened my first business. I opened a restaurant the same week our first child was born. I was working seven days a week trying to get this new restaurant open while trying to be a good husband and a new father. The restaurant was an overnight success, which only whet my appetite for more of this same "drink." Over the next few years I opened two more restaurants, a financial planning office, and—with four other partners—a radio station.

Then at twenty-nine years old, through a series of events, God got my attention, and I walked away from the business world and into pastoral ministry. But instead of working less . . . I started working even more. My home church elected me as their new senior pastor, but the congregation was so split that I was only chosen by a margin of one vote, which basically meant half of my parishioners didn't want me as their pastor. Not exactly an overwhelming vote of approval. (That will hurt a fragile ego.) I then felt this overwhelming need to prove my worth or to prove I had what it took to be a senior pastor.

It was a smaller church of a few hundred people with only one other staff member, which meant I had to do most things myself. My first year as pastor I would start my day leading a 6:00 a.m. prayer meeting, and my day would end at about nine or ten o'clock each night. My kids were still in bed when I left in the morning and were already back in bed before I returned home at night. I worked six days a week and about fifteen hours a day.

After the first year I had not taken any vacation time, so Sandy convinced me to take off a few days so we could drive down to see her sister. I was so physically and emotionally exhausted I slept the entire time we were there. Even when everyone would load up in the car to go somewhere, I would fall asleep in the back seat. Needless to say, Sandy was frustrated.

I had convinced myself that all of these hours I was working were for God, so I didn't see any of it as a problem. But when we got home from that trip, Sandy said, "Steve, if this is ministry, I no longer want any part of it." That was a huge wake-up call for me. I knew I had to make some changes or I was going to lose my family. It was then that I began to realize God was not pleased with the way I was managing my life or my family.

Things got better after that and have continued to improve over the years. But I need to be honest and say that the number of hours I work is still a bit of a struggle for me. For instance, when Sandy leaves town for any short trip, you will never hear her say, "Steve, please don't go to a bar while I am gone." But you will hear her say, "Steve, please don't work like a madman the entire time I'm gone." So even though things have greatly improved, I still work a lot of hours.

A workaholic is someone who works compulsively. You will find them in every possible occupation, and they are usually very successful. Unfortunately, their success only increases their hunger for more. In sales, they are generally the top salesperson. In sports, they are always high achievers. In academics, they are commonly at the top of the class. For them the only thing that energizes them is work.

Addiction Now states, "Workaholism affects about 10 percent of American workers and has been clinically associated with multiple negative events, such as domestic conflicts, insomnia, physical and mental health concerns, and a dissatisfaction with one's life."[2]

Addictions are divided into two broad categories: substance addiction and behavioral addiction. Substance addiction is when you are addicted to a substance like alcohol or drugs. Behavioral addictions consist of compulsive behaviors that if not dealt with can take over someone's life.

Most addictions have a stigma that goes along with them, and no one wants to be known as an addict. But workaholism is different. It seems to be the most respectable sin in the Christian community. I know for me, instead of being embarrassed about it, I've often been guilty of wearing it like a badge of honor. I have always wanted people to know that I work a lot. As is the case with most workaholics, I have struggled with insecurity and thought working long hours would cause people to look up to me or admire me. Therefore, the more I've worked, the better I've felt about myself.

But please don't get me wrong. I'm not suggesting that you refrain from working hard—far from it! The Bible tells us the importance of developing a solid work ethic. God wants us to be hard workers. In fact, I think Christians should be the best workers in any work environment, from the air conditioned office to the construction site. They should have the best attitudes, be the most dependable, and demonstrate the most integrity. That's what Paul meant when he said, "Whatever you do, work at it with all your heart, as working for the Lord" (Col. 3:23 NIV). In fact, I believe God has you in your place of employment for more than a paycheck. Your primary responsibility is to model Christ so you can influence those you work with.

So then, what's the difference between a hard worker and a workaholic? It has a lot to do with what's driving us. While the hard worker may put in long hours, they are still emotionally present for all family members, coworkers, and friends. They manage to maintain a healthy balance between work and personal responsibility, and they enjoy outside activities when they have free time.

On the other hand, workaholics value work over any other

activity, even when it negatively affects their health and family. They typically have no outside interests or activities and their work has become an obsession.

And today's digital world adds a whole new dimension to the concept of workaholism. We have Wi-Fi, smartphones, laptops, and tablets providing the opportunity to work from anywhere at any time. With this new ability to work from home, it blurs the lines between work and relaxation even more. If Sandy and I are at home in the evening, we will often watch television together. The entire time I typically have my laptop open answering e-mails until I go to bed.

There is a story about a little boy who goes to his mother and says, "Mommy, why does Daddy bring a briefcase full of work home every night so that he never has time to play with me?"

The mother tries to explain. "Honey, you have to understand. Daddy can't get all of his work done at work, so he has to bring it home in the evenings."

The little boy looks up at his mother and says, "If he can't get all of his work done, why don't they put him in a slower class?"

If you are a workaholic, you are always spinning plates. You work while you are at home, you work on the weekends, and you work while you're on vacation (if anyone can get you to even take a vacation).

Listen, you may accomplish a lot in your life. You may be running hard from early morning until late at night. But are you taking time for God, slowing down enough for him to work on your soul? Or are you so wrapped up in your work that you are missing out on the things that matter most? You may be successful and even influential, you may dine in the best restaurants and take incredible trips, you might be a leader in the business world who can cut deals in your sleep, but perhaps your soul feels spiritually dead. The reality is that nothing of enduring value happens at Mach speed.

In the *Harvard Business Review* Nancy Rothbard writes about the medical research conducted with more than seven hundred employees. What they found is that it was not the work hours that caused the health issues; it was the workaholism. Again, those are not one and the same. The research showed that employees who worked more than forty hours a week but did not obsess about work reported fewer health complaints than workaholics. "Workaholics, whether or not they worked long hours, reported more health complaints and had increased risk for metabolic syndrome; they also reported a higher need for recovery, more sleep problems, more cynicism, more emotional exhaustion, and more depressive feelings than employees who merely worked long hours but did not have workaholic tendencies."[3]

The University of Bergen developed the Bergen Work Addiction Scale. It's widely accepted by the medical community and measures a number of factors based on how closely they apply to a person's life. The items are rated on a scale of:

never (1)
rarely (2)
sometimes (3)
often (4)
always (5)

Items you may be asked to rate include:

- You think of how you can free up more time to work.
- You work in order to reduce guilt, helplessness, depression, and anxiety.

- You've been told to reduce your time working but ignore those requests.
- You spend much more time working than you initially intend.
- You become stressed when you are not able to work.
- You lower the importance of hobbies, fun activities, and fitness in exchange for more work time.
- You work so much that it has negatively impacted your health.

Research related to the scale published in the *Scandinavian Journal of Psychology* indicates that if you can answer "often" or "always" to at least four of these items, you may have a work addiction.[4]

So what about you? Do four or more apply? If so, what are you going to do to break this bad habit and put some balance back in your life? Remember, workaholism has more to do with your heart. It's a good indicator that work has become an idol in your life, that it's become more important to you than your relationship with God. If workaholism has become an issue, you need to take steps to eliminate it from your life. Let's look at what you can do to break this bad habit and move toward a healthier life.

Own It

Despite the fact that we live in a culture that normalizes or even champions overwork, workaholism is a very real problem. The effects of it can be devastating not only to the families of those who struggle with it, but oftentimes to their employees who are then expected to follow the same overworked schedules. And sooner or later it will harm your health.

Just as in the twelve-step approach developed by Alcoholics Anonymous, the first step used by Workaholics Anonymous is "Admitting you have no control over your relationship with work and acknowledging that working too much is making your life unmanageable."[5] Take the first step to acknowledge you have a problem. Then make the decision to take the necessary steps to solve it.

It might come as a surprise to you when you recognize you are a workaholic, but it certainly won't come as a surprise to your family or coworkers. They've known it for quite a while. And that is the real impact of workaholism: it leaves very little time for our personal lives and often causes our relationships outside of work to disintegrate.

The first step to breaking the bad habit of workaholism is to acknowledge that you have an unhealthy relationship with work that is undermining the important relationships in your life. Once you have acknowledged it, take these steps to put things back in perspective and to start enjoying life outside of work.

Steps to a Godly Habit

STEP 1: CHANGE YOUR MINDSET

Most workaholics believe that their work must take priority in their lives. You need to change that way of thinking. While the workplace should certainly be important to us, it should in no way be as important as our relationships with God and our family.

Workaholics often find their significance or identity in their job or in what they do: "I am an attorney" or "I am a plumber" or "I am a teacher." But that's what you do, not who you are. So ask yourself, "Who am I?" And if you come up with anything other than, "I am a Christian," you have a false identity and need to change your mindset. Friends, if you are a believer, you are a child of God, a Christian. That's who you are.

STEP 2: SET HEALTHY BOUNDARIES

This is hard, and I'm still not great at it, but it's important to establish a work schedule that is healthy and try to stick to it. If you need to include a few late evenings or weekend hours, that's all right, but make a decision that they must be scheduled meetings on your calendar rather than deciding at the last minute to stay late. Make a commitment to go home at a fixed time each day. In other words, learn to say no and walk away.

STEP 3: ADOPT GOD'S RHYTHM OF LIFE

At creation, we see that God worked six days and then took a day of rest. In so doing, he was creating a rhythm to life. He was showing us how to engage and then withdraw, how there is a time for work and a time for rest. It was so important that he made it a part of his Ten Commandments. The fourth commandment is to "Remember to observe the Sabbath day by keeping it holy. You have six days each week for your ordinary work, but the seventh day is a Sabbath day of rest dedicated to the Lord your God. On that day no one in your household may do any work" (Ex. 20:8–10).

Some would argue that God did not create anything on the seventh day, but I would tell you that he created *rest*. But why? Do you think he was tired and needed a break? No, I don't think God gets tired, but I do think he knew we would need that rhythm in our life. We would need a day to step away from work, a day where we remember we are not a human *doing* but a human *being*, a day to reconnect with our Creator.

Even Jesus followed this rhythm of life and took a day of rest every seven days, and he never felt guilty about it. It's as if God was saying, "Six days you run, you labor, and you work hard, but the seventh day is a day to unplug. On the seventh day you remember that the reason you were put on this earth is to be in a relationship with *me*."

Now I'm going to make a statement that will shock you if you are a workaholic: I believe an unbalanced life might just be our greatest sin. When your life is out of balance, you are more impatient, more easily frustrated, and more overwhelmed by problems. When you are tired it's harder for you to connect with your family and harder to get along with people. When you feel more stressed you lose your sense of humor and take life way too seriously. When you are living outside of the God-designed rhythm of life, God takes a back seat when it comes to your priorities.

He says that every seven days you need to build this mini-vacation right into your rhythm of life to keep your body and soul healthy. No matter who you are, you need that day in your week to refresh and renew your body, soul, and spirit. As a pastor, I work weekends, so my day of rest is Friday. If someone asks me for a Friday appointment, I don't need to explain that it's my day off or what I'm doing, I simply say I'm sorry, but I'm already scheduled on Friday. I have zero responsibilities on that day other than to rest, have fun, and be with my wife.

STEP 4: SCHEDULE FAMILY HOLIDAYS

If you don't schedule family vacation time with your kids, then busy schedules will never allow for it. At the beginning of the year I pencil in which weekends I will take off and which weeks I will vacation with my family. When I first started doing it years ago, I thought, *How pathetic that I have to schedule it*. But I now realize that if I don't control my calendar, my calendar will control me. Make sure you block out time for the people who matter the most in your life.

In fact, I would say if you are going to waste time, waste it with the people you care about the most. Think about it. If you only have so much time to spare, don't spend it around the watercooler with the guys at work; spend it with the people you love. Because then it's not really wasted time!

STEP 5: MAKE TIME FOR A HOBBY

Sandy and I don't have a lot of hobbies, but we have worked hard to find things we enjoy doing together. For instance, we both like to go to movies, we like to play pickleball, we love to sit by a pool and read, we like to take walks and ride bikes, we like to work jigsaw puzzles and play cards, and we are both food snobs. You might be surprised at how a couple of hours of activities that you both enjoy will not only recharge your batteries but also strengthen your relationship. So whatever it is you like to do, schedule time for it every week.

STEP 6: CONFRONT YOUR FEARS AND INSECURITIES

There are a lot of different reasons for being a workaholic, but one of them is the fear of loss, the fear of what might happen if you don't work long hours. Fear that you won't make enough money or fear that you won't be liked or looked up to. Insecurity drives a lot of people into workaholism. It's that subtle need for acceptance or approval that we think will come from our work instead of from who we are in Christ.

Ask yourself, Why has work become such a priority? Are you striving for success so people will like or respect you? True self-worth can only be fulfilled by our heavenly Father. God's love and acceptance is not based on what you do and achieve but upon what Jesus Christ has already accomplished for us.

Of course, anytime you are trying to break an addiction or bad habit, accountability is huge. I would encourage you to share your struggle with an accountability partner, a friend, or a spouse, and give that person permission to hold you accountable and to speak into your life concerning this area. The health of your relationship with God as well as your relationships with your family are well worth it.

When you wake up in the morning, what's the first thing that comes to your mind? Do you think about work and what you need to accomplish that day? Or do you think about your relationship with God? I want God to be the first thing I focus on. If you are struggling with workaholism, decide today you are going to take the necessary steps to break this bad habit.

9

LYING

Things come apart so easily when
they are held together with lies.

—Dorothy Allison

Let me just be completely honest and tell you that in my lifetime I have told my fair share of lies. This is hard for me to admit because I don't consider myself a liar.

When I was fifteen, I heard there was a job opening for two people driving an ice cream truck called the Jolly Roger. They not only sold ice cream bars but soft serve as well. I really wanted that job. The only problem was I didn't have a driver's license.

I interviewed for the job and told the owner of the truck I didn't have a license but that my cousin Wes, who was also looking for a job, did. The owner said, "If your cousin wants the job, I will hire you both." While Wes had a driver's license, he didn't know how to drive a manual 4-speed transmission. I didn't have a license, but I knew how to drive manual. I told

Wes there was no way the owner would ever know it was me driving the truck.

But then the first night of our shift we were shocked when the owner showed up to see us off. Fortunately, the truck was parked on a hill, so Wes got behind the wheel and pushed in the clutch, which allowed the truck to coast down to the bottom of the hill, out of the sight of our employer. Once we got to the bottom of the hill, I slid into the driver's seat and drove the rest of the shift. We only had that job for about a month before the owner let us go (we didn't make any money because we kept eating all the profits), but he never suspected that we had lied to him.

There are several more examples of times I was less than honest. I've never been a compulsive liar or an embezzler or a thief, but I have certainly been less than honest when I found it convenient.

I believe most people have told a lie at one time or another. Maybe you twisted the truth to keep from hurting someone or misled an individual to achieve something you wanted or exaggerated or embellished a story. While you might not define yourself as a liar, I would imagine you have told a few.

Unfortunately, most people no longer think of lying as that big of a deal. I mean, it's a part of life, right? We don't get upset when someone exaggerates, falsifies, fabricates, misrepresents, glosses over, or tells a little white lie. We live in a day where we have been bombarded with falsified résumés, overstated ads, erased tapes, loopholes, and cover-ups. We see it in politics, in marriage, in tax returns, on the internet, on social media, and even in conversations with friends. Pamela Meyer, author of *Liespotting*, claimed in her TED Talk that we're facing a pandemic of deception. She says we are lied to between ten and two hundred times a day.[1]

In the movie *Something's Gotta Give* there's a scene where Diane Keaton catches the man she loves (Jack Nicholson) out on a date with another woman. He pleads with her, "I have never lied to you, I have always told you some version of the truth." She replies, "The truth doesn't have versions, okay?"

A *Psychology Today* article says that "the truth may have many sides to it. It may be complicated or hard to understand, but it exists . . . in one version. . . . It's common for people to only mention the parts of the truth that they feel are acceptable or that they think people want to hear, leaving the full truth hidden away."[2]

Several years ago, the Leo Burnett advertising agency did a telephone survey on lying. The results were interesting. Ninety-one percent of those interviewed said they regularly lied. Seventy-nine percent had given out false phone numbers or invented new identities when meeting strangers on airplanes. Twenty percent admitted they couldn't get through one day without going along with a previously manufactured lie. Can you guess what we lie about the most? Our weight![3]

I find that funny because your weight is the one thing that you can't conceal! I had a business partner who was extremely heavy. He and I were at the airline counter buying tickets for a short flight on a small prop plane. The ticket agent asked each of us how much we weighed. When my friend gave his weight, I knew it wasn't true. I turned toward him and said, "Buddy, now is not the time to lie about your weight!"

In that same survey the Leo Burnett agency also found that money was the second most common thing people lied about; the third thing was our age. I read a story about a woman who introduced her thirty-five-year-old daughter as only twenty-four. Later the girl asked her mother why she had lied about her age.

The mother said, "I realized I had been lying about my own age for so long that I would have to lie about your age for it to make any sense!"

People have simply come to expect that politicians, lawyers, lobbyists, journalists, talk-show hosts, and anyone else in the public view will lie if it serves their purpose. Teachers just expect to hear "My dog ate my homework." Policemen expect to hear "My speedometer is off."

But God hates lying. In fact Proverbs 6 lists seven things God hates and two of them refer to dishonesty, "There are six things the Lord hates—no, seven things he detests: haughty eyes, a lying tongue, hands that kill the innocent, a heart that plots evil, feet that race to do wrong, a false witness who pours out lies, a person who sows discord in a family" (Prov. 6:16–19).

Why is God so opposed to lying? Because it is so contrary to his very nature. Look at how Jesus described his character. "I am the way and the truth and the life. No one comes to the Father except through me" (John 14:6 NIV). He didn't say, "I speak truth." He said, "I *am* truth." In other words, he didn't conform to some standard of truth—he *is* the standard. It's not that God has decided he will not lie. He cannot lie because anything he says will come into being, even if it didn't exist before he said it. And so as his people we are called to exemplify Christ by making truth a priority.

And yet on the other hand, Jesus cuts right to the chase when he refers to the evil one. "He has always hated the truth, because there is no truth in him. When he lies, it is consistent with his character; for he is a liar and the father of lies" (John 8:44). I've heard it said that "a man is never more like the devil than when he's telling a lie." In Proverbs it says, "The Lord detests lying lips, but he delights in people who are trustworthy" (12:22 NIV).

It's important to understand that lying comes in many different forms.

Deception

Mark Twain was right when he said, "If you tell the truth you don't have to remember anything."[4] Lies paint you into a corner because you now have to live in this false little world you have created. You have to keep track of every lie and whom you told it to. Paul said it pretty clearly, "So stop telling lies. Let us tell our neighbors the truth, for we are all parts of the same body" (Eph. 4:25).

That's why it's so important to be truthful with one another, because healthy relationships are built on trust. A husband lies to his wife when he tells her he's working late but actually goes to the bar with his buddies. She finds out that he's lied, and instantly that foundation of trust in their relationship has been damaged. She starts to wonder if she can trust anything he has ever told her. And while they can work out their troubles, it may take months if not years to reestablish that same level of trust they once shared before this one lie damaged it.

There can be a lot of reasons why we might want to deceive someone. One reason would be to get revenge. At the first church I pastored there was a middle-aged man in our church accused by a young teenage girl of touching her inappropriately. We discovered later she had a crush on him, but he ignored her. This made her mad and she later admitted to her parents that she made the story up because she was angry at him for ignoring her. I can tell you this young girl's lie was devastating to this man and his wife!

What's ironic about deception is that we will actually tell a lie because we want people to think the best of us. The deceiver tries to create an impression that misleads people by not telling all the facts or by creating a false impression. He doesn't want people to know he made a mistake so he will make a bigger mistake of trying to cover it up.

- The check is in the mail.
- We service what we sell.
- Give me your number and he will call you right back.
- Your luggage isn't lost; it is just misplaced.
- Leave your résumé and we will keep it on file.
- I just need five minutes of your time.
- Open wide. It won't hurt!

Whenever or however we distort the truth, it's a lie.

Gossip

It has become an epidemic in our culture today. You hear it in homes, around the office, at parties, on social media, and in the tabloids. It has become a booming industry that is taking over our media. Accusations or hearsay are shared without any proof or evidence, destroying people's credibility and lives. The standard has become if enough people whisper it, then it must be true. You hear people say things like, "I don't believe it's true, but I hear . . ." or "I probably shouldn't tell you, but I know it won't go any further . . ." or "Don't tell anybody, but I heard . . ." Proverbs 20:19 says, "A gossip goes around telling secrets, so don't hang around with chatterers."

Unfortunately, many Christians will spread gossip packaged as a prayer request: "I'm only telling you this so you will pray . . ." Friends, no matter how spiritual you try to make it sound, when you repeat gossip it's wrong.

There was once a rumor in the newspaper that the great American writer Mark Twain had died. Twain responded to a reporter who questioned him about it, writing, "The report of my death was an exaggeration."[5] Most of us are like the guy who said, "I just want my friends to know it's not me who starts all of those rumors . . . it's the people I tell them to!" Gossip damages reputations and relationships.

Self-Protection

This is the person who lies to protect himself from getting in trouble. "I thought I was going sixty-five, officer," claims the driver who was going eighty. "I thought the assignment was due this Friday," claims the student who knew it was due on Wednesday but didn't get it finished.

In the Old Testament, Joseph's brothers were so jealous of him that they actually sold him into slavery. But they later lied to their father by telling him that Joseph was killed and eaten by a wild animal. They were protecting themselves because they knew their father would be outraged if he discovered what they had done.

I'm sure we've all lied as children to keep from getting in trouble. It's cute when a little boy with chocolate all over his face stands in front of his parents and says, "I didn't eat the chocolate-chip cookies." But it's no longer cute when he does it as a teenager.

There is an old adage that says, "Sin has many tools, but a lie is the handle that fits them all."

Cheating

The cheater lies to get an advantage. When a student cheats on a test, he is lying to his teacher. When a salesperson writes down more expenses than he incurred, he is lying to his employer. When someone falsifies expenses on his tax return, he is lying to the government.

Flattery

This is when you tell someone what you think will make him feel good to gain an advantage for yourself. Most people are wise to it, but it's easy to fall for this type of deception. Proverbs says, "A lying tongue hates its victims, and flattering words cause ruin" (26:28).

Exaggeration

When you exaggerate you overstate the truth to look good or to convince someone to do something you want. Maybe you are upset with a neighbor, so you go to him and say, "I think you need to know that most of the neighbors are upset about this." Or you overstate your experience on your résumé or hyperbolize what someone has done to you. To exaggerate takes the truth and turns it into an untruth.

Silence

Maybe you hear something that you know is not true, but you remain silent. To know the truth and not speak up is a form of lying; it's complicity by passivity. Or maybe you're on a diet and the doctor asks what you've been eating. You tell him some of the things you've eaten, but you don't mention the cream cheese bagel you had at breakfast. Leaving out significant facts starts a habit of silent deception.

Broken Promises

"For the LORD your God demands that you promptly fulfill all your vows, or you will be guilty of sin" (Deut. 23:21). We don't think about breaking a promise as being a lie, but it is. Whether it's a promise to pay a debt, a promise to take your kids to the zoo, or a promise to be faithful to your spouse, when you don't keep your word, it's a lie. I heard one person define integrity as doing what you say you are going to do. God tells us not to bear false witness, to be people of truth, to be honest to the core, and to always do what you say you are going to do.

Omission

You might say to someone, "I didn't lie to you; I just didn't tell you." While you might not have told them a lie, by purposely leaving out important information, you have misled them. When you fail to correct a preexisting misconception to conceal the truth, that is deception.

Maybe someone asks you out on a date. You later discover this person is married. You are angry and ask them why they didn't tell you. Their response is simply that you didn't ask. In my case the owner of the ice cream truck believed Wes was driving, and I didn't tell him otherwise. Since he didn't ask, I didn't tell. I allowed him to believe an untruth. I didn't feel any guilt because I justified in my mind that I had not lied to him. But my failure to tell my employer that I was driving could have caused a serious problem. If I would have had an accident—or worse yet run over a child—my employer as well as my parents could have been held responsible for something they didn't even know was happening.

Maybe you didn't want to hurt someone's feelings or you were worried that if they knew the truth it might break their heart, that if you spoke up about a misconception they might not go through with their decision. While you might justify your silence as well-intentioned, it is lying nonetheless, and when the truth eventually comes out, it can be a detriment to your relationship.

There is an old saying I'm sure you've heard: honesty is the best policy. The reason everyone has heard it is because it's such a true statement. While some habits are worse than others, I believe lying is right up there at the top. If we ignore it, it will become a habit and begin to feel more comfortable than telling the truth. Lying is destructive and will eventually lead to painful consequences. It will hinder your personal as well as your spiritual development. And it will cause you to fall short of God's plan for your life. That's why getting control of it is critical.

Own It

Listen, every destructive habit leads to painful consequences. And yet if we don't break this habit of lying, none of the other chapters in this book will matter. Because when we choose to lie, it will lead to pain in our lives. It will also lead to embarrassment when someone confronts us with our lies. Think how much better off we would be if we would just break the habit of lying.

To have someone call you a liar feels very offensive. We quickly declare that we are not a liar and come up with several excuses as to why we told that lie. And yet if we are telling lies, then we are in fact a liar. And when you make poor choices, there will be consequences. Consequences to the relationships that matter most in your life.

But if you are serious about breaking this habit, the first step you need to take is to own it, to acknowledge it, to admit that lying has become a problem for you. Mark Twain once said, "A man is never more truthful than when he acknowledges himself as a liar."[6]

While admitting a lie is difficult, it's far better than being a compulsive liar.

Steps to a Godly Habit

STEP 1: DO DAMAGE CONTROL

Once you take responsibility for lying, then you need to confess it to God. After all, he has heard every lie you've ever told. And I would start each day by asking God to give you the strength to always tell the truth. "The temptations in your life are no different from what others experience. And God is faithful. He will not allow the temptation to be more than you can stand. When you are tempted, he will show you a way out so that you can endure" (1 Cor. 10:13).

I would also encourage you to ask God to show you if there has been someone you have misled lately or some deception that still needs to be addressed. If there is, I would encourage you to go to those people and make it right. Decide from today forward that if you ever tell a lie, you will go back and admit it to the person you deceived. "I just need to restate something I said to you earlier that was not exactly truthful." "I need you to know that I misspoke when I explained that to you earlier." This is hard and humbling, but making this commitment will cause you to think twice before you tell another lie.

STEP 2: TAME THE TONGUE

Scripture has a lot to say about our speech, most of it about the need to control it. If you genuinely want God's best in your life, honesty is not just the best policy—it's the only policy that will honor God. "For the Scriptures say, 'If you want to enjoy life and see many happy days, keep your tongue from speaking evil and your lips from telling lies'" (1 Peter 3:10).

If you can control your tongue, you will have control over yourself. If you have ever been in a tight spot or felt the pressure of the moment, it's easy to base your response on how you think it will affect the outcome. So when confronted you need to make a conscious decision to tell the truth regardless of the anticipated consequences.

As I have already pointed out, your tongue is a significant

player in your walk with the Lord. In the New Testament, the book of James says, "Indeed, we all make many mistakes. For if we could control our tongues, we would be perfect and could also control ourselves in every other way. We can make a large horse go wherever we want by means of a small bit in its mouth. And a small rudder makes a huge ship turn wherever the pilot chooses to go, even though the winds are strong" (3:2–4). Just as a horse needs a bit in its mouth to control the direction it goes, we need to control our tongues. Having free rein with our speech is not biblical, even if we think we are being honest.

STEP 3: SPEAK THE TRUTH LOVINGLY

While some people are very honest, they are also insensitive to people's feelings. The Bible clearly says, "We will speak the truth in love, growing in every way more and more like Christ" (Eph. 4:15). Love has got to be our filter—love for God and love for others. It's like the fourth-grade class that sent a card to the teacher who had been absent recovering from a surgery. They said, "Dear Ms. Fisher, Your fourth-grade class wishes you a speedy recovery by a vote of 15–14." The problem with children is not that they are too honest, it's that they just haven't learned to speak the truth in love.

At the end of the day people may not remember exactly what you said, and people will forget what you did, but people will never forget how you made them feel.

STEP 4: DEVELOP ACCOUNTABILITY

When you decide to break this habit of lying, you may have the best of intentions, but if no one is holding you accountable, it's easy to fall back into the same old pattern of deception. You see, accountability and execution are linked. Accountability provides you with guardrails to keep you on the road to recovery. So find a friend who is willing to hold you accountable, someone who is willing to ask you the tough questions:

- Have you lied to anyone this week?
- Have you spread gossip about anyone?
- Have you exaggerated?
- Have you cheated in any way?
- Have you used flattery to get your way?
- Have you misled anyone?

STEP 5: UNDERSTAND THE PRESSURE TO LIE

There are several things that can make us feel the pressure to lie. So ask yourself, "Why is this situation so important to me that I'm willing to lie about it? What am I trying to hide from?" And then ask God to help you understand why you keep lying. Here are several examples of why we can feel the pressure to lie:

1. Addicts will lie to cover up their addiction. Wrong actions almost always lead to lies.
2. People are afraid of not being liked or they don't want to disappoint someone, so they will say what they think others want to hear.
3. Greed can cause people to lie. We want something, so we will say what we need to say to get what we want. Why study for a test when you can cheat? Why follow the rules in a business transaction when a little exaggeration can close the deal much quicker?

4. Losing control can tempt you to lie to regain control of the situation.
5. And lies can snowball. We tell a little lie, but then to cover that lie we tell a bigger one. Then another one is required to keep the deception going, and another one after that. An admission would cause the entire house of cards to come tumbling down, so you just keep lying. But regardless of what is causing you to feel pressure to lie, in the end it will bite you if you don't stop.

STEP 6: PRACTICE INTEGRITY IN ALL THINGS

Jesus told the parable of the shrewd manager and then at the end said, "If you are faithful in little things, you will be faithful in large ones. But if you are dishonest in little things, you won't be honest with greater responsibilities" (Luke 16:10).

If you are going to break this habit of lying, you have to be truthful in every area of your life. Not just in the big things, but in the everyday choices you make as well. Decide that you are going to be a person of integrity in every area of your life.

Regardless what our culture thinks, lying is a serious problem. God hates it and so should we. The truth may not always be easy to tell, but in the long run you will earn a lot more trust and respect from the people who matter most. Like any bad habit, it's not easy to stop lying, but if you want people to trust you, it's certainly necessary.

10

IDOLATRY

There are more idols in the world
than there are realities.

—Friedrich Nietzsche,
Twilight of the Idols

The human heart is an idol factory.

—Tim Keller

As I write this chapter, we are in day twenty-eight of a stay-at-home order. The coronavirus first surfaced in a seafood and poultry market in Wuhan, China, in late December 2019. The pandemic has expanded to touch nearly every corner of the globe. On March 11, 2020, the Trump administration announced the restriction of travel from Europe to the United States for thirty days in an attempt to slow the spread of the virus. A few days later the president declared a national emergency. And by the end of

March the Senate reached an agreement on a $2 trillion stimulus deal, the most expensive and far-reaching such measure in the history of Congress. It was determined that most Americans would receive a check to offset the economic damage caused by businesses closing during this time.

Everything we thought we would be doing during this season looked vastly different than we had expected, and the feelings of loss have been very real. Our world has been rocked by the coronavirus.

During this social distancing season, I've heard a few people question why God hasn't stopped this pandemic. The question reminds me of the response Billy Graham's daughter, Anne Graham Lotz, gave during an interview on CBS's *Early Show.* It was the Thursday after the September 11, 2001, terrorist attacks, and Jane Clayson asked, "I've heard people say, those who are religious, those who are not, if God is good, how could God let this happen? To that, you say?"

Anne replied:

> I say God is also angry when he sees something like this. I would say also for several years now Americans in a sense have shaken their fist at God and said, God, we want you out of our schools, our government, our business, we want you out of our marketplace. And God, who is a gentleman, has just quietly backed out of our national and political life, our public life. Removing his hand of blessing and protection. We need to turn to God first of all and say, God, we're sorry we have treated you this way and we invite you now to come into our national life. We put our trust in you. We have our trust in God on our coins, we need to practice it.[1]

While we have all faced challenges during this pandemic, we have also experienced a great spiritual awakening. Winston Churchill once said, "Never let a good crisis go to waste."[2] And for sure God is up to something. I don't believe that God caused this crisis, but I do believe he is using it to bring a spiritual awareness in America. With worshipers confined to their homes, and church doors closed, the number of people watching church services on livestream is greater than ever before. People are anxious and searching for answers. For instance, I've heard that Bible sales have dramatically increased. And what millions have discovered is a relationship with God.

One of the ways God got our attention was to expose the idols in our lives. We don't think of there being idols in the twenty-first century, but idolatry is actually a common problem in our world today. Tim Keller defines an idol as "anything more important to you than God, anything that absorbs your heart and imagination more than God, anything you seek to give you what only God can give."[3] I love that: "anything that absorbs your heart and imagination more than God."

During the COVID-19 crisis we saw potential idols stripped away in a matter of a few days as most states issued stay-at-home orders.

Independence: It felt like overnight all of our personal freedoms to go where we wanted and do what we wanted were restricted.

Academics: Schools and universities across America were canceled through the end of the school year.

Money: The economy tanked as businesses barely survived or were forced to shut down. And by March 23, 2020, the stock market had seen a decline of 35 percent from its February record.

Sports: Nearly every major sporting event in the United States was suspended or canceled, including the 2020 Summer Olympics.

Travel: Leisure and short-term vacation plans became almost nonexistent. (Southwest e-mailed me to let me know an upcoming flight to Florida was canceled.)

Entertainment: Hollywood and Broadway shut down. Movie theaters were shuttered. Disney World and other theme parks all closed. Restaurants and bars were reduced to carry-out only. The entire entertainment world was nonfunctional.

Politics: With 2020 being an election year, sixteen states postponed their primaries, and campaign rallies from both parties were canceled.

Religion: Churches across America closed their doors and instead streamed their services online.

Science: Modern medicine struggled to come up with a vaccine to fight the virus. They were unsure how to help dying patients.

Now please understand there is nothing inherently wrong with any of the things that were taken away from us. But while they often garner our affection, they cannot meet the needs of our destitute heart, which is why Jesus said, "Seek the Kingdom of God above all else, and live righteously, and he will give you everything you need" (Matt. 6:33).

What is an idol? It's anything in the created order that we exchange for the Creator. Or you could say it's disordered affections. Here is how Paul described idols in Romans: "They exchanged the truth about God for a lie, and worshiped and served created things rather than the Creator—who is forever praised" (1:25 NIV). Instead of loving God with all of our hearts, we love created things, and consequently our affections are out of order.

Biblically, we call those things idols, but psychologically we call them addictions or habits. An idol is an addiction or bad habit you have formed in your life. It has become a habit because of the importance you have placed on it, and the thought of letting it go strikes fear in you. Paul wrote, "You know the way you lived before you were believers. You let yourselves be influenced and led away to worship idols—things that could not speak" (1 Cor. 12:2 NCV). If you ignore this habit, not only will it hurt your relationship with God, but it will begin to consume your time, your money, your energy, your affection, and your thought life.

The reason an idol has so much power over us is, as we saw earlier, we have allowed it to absorb our heart and imagination more than God. We have become so attached to this thing that our very existence feels dependent on it. It can be anything from your love of sports, to a habit of spending money, gaming, food, your phone, your job, or a relationship. I could go on and on. Thousands of things can capture your heart and dominate your life—your bad habits are the idols in your life.

I know idolatry feels like an obsolete term that conjures up pictures of primitive people bowing down before statues. But idolatry is a major theme of the Bible and is just as relevant today as it was in the first century. More than fifty of the laws in the first five books of the Bible are aimed at idolatry. It was one of only four sins to which the death penalty was attached. The first two of the Ten Commandments deal directly with idolatry. If idolatry is that big of an issue in Scripture, don't you think we should pay attention to the warnings?

While idolatry is mentioned all throughout Scripture, the reference that immediately comes to my mind is when Moses came off the mountain with the Ten Commandments in Exodus 20. The first three commandments guide our relationship with God.

1. You shall have no other gods before me.
2. You shall make no idols.
3. You shall not take the name of the Lord your God in vain.

He didn't give us these first three commandments because he wanted to be the first among many gods in our lives. He gave us these commandments because he wanted to be the *only* God in our lives. He would not tolerate the worship of other gods as was a common practice in Egypt and other nations. God created us to be in relationship with him and him alone. I love the way Kyle Idleman says it in his book *Gods at War*:

> God declines to sit atop an organizational flowchart. He *is* the organization. He is not interested in being president of the board. He *is* the board. And life doesn't work until everyone else sitting around the table in the boardroom of your heart is fired. He is God, and there are no other applicants for that position. There are no partial gods, no honorary gods, no interim gods, no assistants to the regional gods.
>
> God is saying this not because he is insecure but because it's the way of truth in this universe, which is his creation.

> Only one God owns and operates it. Only one God designed it, and only one God knows how it works. He is the only God who can help us, direct us, satisfy us, save us.[4]

God created us to worship him and him alone.

While God was giving Moses the Ten Commandments on Mount Sinai, the people waiting below were complaining because in their mind it was taking too long. They gathered everyone's gold and made a golden calf to worship. When Moses returned and saw their worship of idols, he was so angered at them that he shattered the tablets with the Ten Commandments written on them.

Instead of waiting on their Creator, they decided to make a god of their own creation—at the very same time God was giving Moses the first commandment, "You shall have no other gods before me" (Ex. 20:3 NIV). We must understand that God hates idolatry and is unwilling to share the praise he deserves with another: "I am the LORD; that is my name! I will not give my glory to anyone else, nor share my praise with carved idols" (Isa. 42:8). God is a "jealous" God in the sense that he expects our full devotion, not a partial, lukewarm commitment. God wants us to be all in when it comes to our relationship with him.

There are so many stories in the Old Testament about idolatry, from Elijah as he challenged the prophets of Baal to the three Hebrew teenagers thrown into a fiery furnace by Nebuchadnezzar because they refused to bow a knee to a false idol. But even as you move to the New Testament, idolatry continues to be a theme. Paul said, "Therefore put to death your members which are on the earth: fornication, uncleanness, passion, evil desire, and covetousness, which is idolatry" (Col. 3:5 NKJV). Idolatry is an issue of the heart. Paul tells us that it starts with covetousness. While *covetousness* is a word we may not use much anymore, the evidence of it is seen in idolatry. Covetousness is noticeable by an excessive desire for wealth or possessions. It diverts your attention away from God toward something else.

As I said, we live in a time where people put other things before God. Let me give you a couple of examples.

Think about your cell phone. According to RescueTime, most people spend three hours and fifteen minutes a day on their phones. That's just the average. The top 20 percent of smartphone users spend more than four and a half hours a day on their phones. On average, RescueTime users check their phones fifty-eight times during the day, with thirty instances taking place during work hours.[5]

It's clear that excessive cell phone use is a growing problem. At the end of 2019, Pew Research Center reported that 81 percent of Americans owned smartphones; in 2011, it was only 35 percent. Google Trends shows that searches for "cell phone addiction" have also been on the rise over the past five years. "The dangers of using a cell phone while driving are widely known, yet people ignore the risk in pursuit of the small jolt of connectedness a phone provides," reported a Healthline article.[6] There's little doubt that cell phone use has become an idol for a lot of people.

Another example of idolatry is sports. I believe sports have become our biggest idol in America. The growing devotion to this god has grown so large it's hard for anyone to deny the love affair we have with sports. Take the National Football League, for example. Since 1972 the NFL has dominated the playing field as the favorite spectator sport of Americans. In 2018 the NFL brought in roughly $16 billion in revenue; from television deals to ticket sales and merchandising, a lot of money changes hands.

Now please understand that I'm not trying to criticize sports or football; I love the game. I'm just observing what is happening when we allow it to become the focus of our passion.

For the last ten years Sandy and I have split season tickets to the Indianapolis Colts with another couple. I really enjoy going to a game. I love the energy in the room when sixty thousand people are all together on their feet cheering on their favorite team with great passion. I love how everyone is either wearing a team jersey, their team colors, or have painted their faces to demonstrate their loyalty to their team. At a game you may not know the people sitting around you, but it doesn't stop you from giving high fives and hugs to everyone nearby when your team scores. And not only is every seat in the house taken, but the fans have paid a lot of money to have that seat. They will gather for three hours and then be excited if the game goes into overtime! Not only will they put up with the crowds and traffic, they might even drive an hour or two just to get to the stadium. And many of them arrive a couple hours early to tailgate with friends before they even go into the game.

One Sunday Sandy and I were late for a 1:00 p.m. game. (The pastor was long-winded that day.) Our parking spot is about four blocks from the stadium, and it was cold, raining, and extremely windy. As Sandy and I were making our way toward the stadium through this extreme weather, I couldn't believe I was willing to go through this just to watch a game. I said to my wife, "I wonder how many Christians would go through these same conditions to get to church." And to think some stadiums are open-air and fans sit outside in subzero weather for three hours to watch the game!

I'm just making the point that we live in a land where sports in general compete for our attention and our affections—all kinds of sports, from playing to watching. It might be football or golf, basketball or swimming, baseball or soccer, running or biking, CrossFit or NASCAR, or any other athletic event. But again, I want to make it clear that sports are not the problem—it's what we have done with them in our lives and how we have allowed them to consume our devotion.

I'm not saying you must take sports out of your life—or money, or fame, or your phone. I'm just saying it's time to identify which things in your life have become idols and to take the necessary steps to get rid of them.

Own It

The first step in breaking free from a habit of idolatry is to identify the things you are putting before God. Is it success? Your spouse? Is it your image? Nothing should come before the Lord. You could start by asking yourself a few of these questions:

- What do you feel like you need to be happy?
- Where do you consistently spend the most money?
- What's the first thing you think about when you wake up in the morning?
- What would you have a hard time letting go of for a month?
- What do you like to talk about?
- What do you gravitate to when you go through struggles in life?
- What do you spend too much time on each day?

If your answer is the same to most of these questions, then it's likely that thing has become an idol. And you need to admit it to yourself. That relationship or that substance or that object has now progressed to the point that it's more important to you than your relationship with God.

Steps to a Godly Habit

STEP 1: WORK ON YOUR RELATIONSHIP WITH GOD

Mankind was created by God to be in fellowship with him, to worship him. Within our soul is this God-sized hole or emptiness that was intended to be filled with a relationship with Christ. On the other hand, we have this independent spirit, or what we call the flesh, that wants to go its own way and do its own thing. So rather than surrender your life to the Lord, you try to fill the emptiness with created things, things that will satisfy you or give you significance, things you can control. The thought is that created things can be more easily controlled than our Creator. These created things become idols in your life. And for a while they will seem to satisfy this void, but eventually those things will leave you just as empty as you were before.

Mankind was created by God to worship something. It's our response to what we value most. Regardless whether it's fortune, fame, or family, none of those things are wrong in themselves, but when they become more important to us than the worship of God, it becomes idolatry. And yet the solution is not always to remove the object of our idolatry. The solution is to grow in our love for the Lord. Since an idol is anything that becomes more important in your life than your relationship with God, change your focus of worship back to Jesus. Paul said, "Christ's love is greater than anyone can ever know, but I pray that you will be able to know that love. Then you can be filled with the fullness of God" (Eph. 3:19 NCV).

C. S. Lewis explained it this way:

> Creatures are not born with desires unless satisfaction for those desires exists. A baby feels hunger . . . well, there is such a thing as food. A duckling wants to swim; there is such a thing as water. . . . If I find in myself a desire which no experience in this world can satisfy, the most probable explanation is that I was made for another world. If none of my earthly pleasures satisfy it, that does not prove the universe is a fraud. Probably earthly pleasures were never meant to satisfy it but only to arouse it, to suggest the real thing.[7]

The more you are in love with God the more it shoves everything else aside and fills that God-sized vacuum with his presence. Paul said, "I want to know Christ and experience the mighty power that raised him from the dead" (Phil. 3:10). When you are in love with Christ, when he is your greatest pleasure, you won't go looking for anything else. You will have no need for idols in your life. And yet you will still be able to enjoy these things in your life for who and what they are.

STEP 2: SET BOUNDARIES

When I married Sandy I entered into a covenant relationship with her. I made a commitment before God, my family, my friends—and more importantly my mother-in-law—to be faithful to her, to love and cherish her, till death do us part. I made a promise that there would be no other women in my life. And, therefore, we established boundaries so that our marriage would remain healthy.

But what if I ignored those boundaries and had an adulterous affair with someone else? It would break her heart and do great damage to our marriage. I would have broken my promise that I was all in when it came to our marriage. And it would also be unacceptable to tell Sandy this woman was not as important to me as she was. Sandy would remind me that I promised there would never be another woman in my life.

And yet if Sandy were to forgive me, it would take work to rebuild a healthy marriage. The first thing we would have to do is reestablish boundaries. Things we would begin to do and things we would not do to protect the health of our marriage.

Well, idolatry is a lot like adultery. When I invited Christ into my life, I entered into a covenant relationship with him. If I was serious about this relationship, I established boundaries, promising to be faithful to him, and to be all in when it came to my commitment to him.

But if I were to allow an idol in my life it would break his heart and do great damage to our relationship because I would be breaking my promise to be faithful to him. It would be unacceptable to tell God that this idol was not as important to me as he was. He would remind me that I promised there would be no other gods in my life.

Of course, God is a forgiving God, but if I wanted my relationship with him to be healthy, I would need to reestablish boundaries by starting to do things on a regular basis, like spending more time with God in prayer and the Word, spending more time in worship and thanksgiving to make sure my heart is focused on him. And then there would be things I would stop doing altogether because they kept me from full devotion to Christ.

Establishing boundaries is not a negative thing; it's actually a declaration of my love and commitment to God. It's a practical way of saying, "I love you, God, with all of my heart, mind, soul, and strength. And I have established some guardrails to keep my focus on you." So begin to make a list of all the boundaries you need to establish to make sure your relationship with Christ is always healthy and free of idols.

STEP 3: PRIORITIZE CONFESSION AND ACCOUNTABILITY

Find a friend, a pastor, or a counselor, someone that you can trust. Ask that person if he or she would be willing to hold you accountable, to be that person who is not afraid to ask you the hard questions. James 5:16 says, "Confess your sins to each other and pray for each other so that you may be healed. The earnest prayer of a righteous person has great power and produces wonderful results."

Once you know who that person is, tell him or her about this idol in your life. We all need someone to help us defeat this habit. The enemy will try to convince you that you can do this on your own, but he's a liar. We are all designed for community. "As iron sharpens iron, so one person sharpens another" (Prov. 27:17 NASB). Accountability is the best way to make sure you break this habit in your life.

STEP 4: MAKE HARD CHOICES

In step 2, I said the solution is not always to remove the object of our idolatry; the solution is to grow in our love for the Lord! And yet I also believe there are times that's not enough. In other words, no matter how hard you try to shift your worship to the Lord, you can't seem to stop the worship of this habit that has a hold on you.

Do you remember the story in the Old Testament we talked about earlier? Moses was coming down from Mount Sinai with the Ten Commandments and discovered the people had created a golden calf that they were worshiping. Moses made the hard choice to destroy this idol by burning it and crushing it into a fine powder, which he poured water over, making a liquid that he forced the people to drink.

They had created this idol from their own gold and silver. Moses could have simply melted it down and given them their gold and silver back. But this act of idolatry was so offensive to God that Moses made the hard choice to even destroy their gold and silver.

There are times when an idol has such a grip on your life that you will need to make the hard decision to remove it altogether. In the Sermon on the Mount, Jesus told men to gouge out their eye to destroy the idol of lust. He said it is better to lose a body part than to go to hell (Matt. 5:29). Now, he doesn't want you to literally gouge out your eye, but he does want you to recognize what a serious problem idolatry can be in your life.

Do you need to make some hard choices in your life?

Have your friends pulled you away from God? Do you need to find some new friends?

Has social media become an idol? Do you need to close your account?

Has lust become an idol? Do you need a filter on your internet?

Has the accumulation of wealth become an idol? Do you need to downsize?

I don't know what decision you need to make. But if this area of your life has become a bad habit and you can't replace it with your love and devotion to God, then you need to make a hard choice. Because, as I said earlier, you can't worship both God and idols.

Jesus gave the example of trying to worship both God and money. He said, "No one can serve two masters. For you will hate one and love the other; you will be devoted to one and despise the other. You cannot serve God and be enslaved to money" (Matt. 6:24).

God richly blesses a faithful singleness of purpose, and there is still a curse over this bad habit of idolatry. Stop making excuses for it. Stop lying about it. Name the idol. Repent of it. Ask for help. You have been purchased with the precious blood of Christ for good works for the blessing and building up of the body of Christ. You have the Spirit of God living inside of you to make you a powerful blessing to others.

11

GUILT

There is unspeakable joy . . . for the
person who knows release from guilt
and the release of forgiveness.

—Stuart Briscoe

Guilt says, "You failed."
Shame says, "You're a failure."
Grace says, "Your failures are forgiven."

—Lecrae

When I was ten years old and in the fifth grade, there was a boy in my class whose mother committed suicide. It was a horrible experience for a little boy to find his mother in the garage with the car idling and a hose running from the exhaust pipe to the driver's side window.

As a ten-year-old it was hard for me to even imagine what it would be like for your mother to take her own life. Max returned to school about a week later. I remember wondering how he would act around the rest of us. I can remember being on the playground, and I noticed he was laughing with the other kids and having a good time. I thought he should be acting sad, so with the immaturity of a ten-year-old boy, I said a very cruel and hurtful thing to him: "You don't even care that your mother is dead!" He immediately burst into tears and ran inside the building. I then felt horrible as I realized I had hurt his feelings.

A few minutes later I was called to the principal's office. Both the principal and my teacher let me know that what I had said to this boy was a horrible thing to say. But they didn't need to worry because I already felt the guilt for what I had said.

I think that is my earliest recollection of struggling with feelings of guilt. But like most people I have had a lot of things throughout the years that I regret or feel guilt over.

When I worked late at night, I felt guilty because I wasn't at home with the kids. When I was at home, I felt guilty because I wasn't at work. I felt guilty because I wasn't a better husband. I felt guilty because I wasn't a better son. When I was on the treadmill and listening to a novel, I felt guilty because I wasn't listening to a leadership book. When we would take a family vacation, I felt guilty for spending the money. I felt guilty that I had clothes in my closet I hadn't worn in a while. I did all the things a pastor should do but I never thought I prayed enough or read my Bible enough. I never felt like I made enough phone calls or visited enough people in the hospital. I felt guilty that I couldn't be in two places at the same time. I felt guilty when I worked and I felt guilty when I relaxed. I pretty much felt guilty about everything.

Feelings of guilt often come because you don't think you measure up to your own high standards or because you did something you think you *shouldn't* have done or failed to do something you think you *should* have done. It's a feeling of shame or regret because of bad conduct or, more often, perceived bad conduct. And you keep yourself in that state of guilt because you think you need to pay for what you did or didn't do.

"I feel bad for not doing that."

"I feel horrible for letting her down."

"I feel like it's my fault."

"I'm mad at myself for not . . ."

If you say things like this, you are probably struggling with guilt.

Through the years my wife has confronted me on several occasions and said, "Steve, you are driven by feelings of guilt, and it's not healthy." Which is why I've always related to David when he wrote in Psalms, "My guilt has overwhelmed me like a burden too heavy to bear. My wounds fester and are loathsome because of my sinful folly. I am bowed down and brought very low; all day long I go about mourning" (38:4–6 NIV).

And yet while I continue to struggle at times with feelings of guilt, I no longer feel like I'm driven by my guilt. It's no longer habitual because I've taken positive steps to let go of it.

I found this startling research published in the *Harvard Business Review*: "People who are prone to guilt tend to work harder and perform better than people who are not guilt-prone, and are perceived to be more capable leaders."[1]

Does that mean that guilt is a good thing? You do need some guilt. If you have never experienced guilt, it could be a sign you are a sociopath or have narcissistic personality disorder, making you one of those rare people who are incapable of feeling guilt or regret.

There are actually two types of guilt. There is the healthy kind that comes from the Holy Spirit. It is intended to lead us to repentance and a return to God's plan for our life. Once we respond to the conviction of the Holy Spirit, that guilt is gone and replaced by God's peace and joy.

The other type of guilt is often called *false guilt*. That's when you have feelings of guilt even though you haven't done anything wrong. Or maybe you *did* do something wrong but have already fixed it and asked God to forgive you—and yet you still feel guilty. False guilt can affect *any* area of your life and keep you trapped in an unhealthy place if you don't do something about it.

Maybe a friend is having marriage problems and they ask if you will come over and talk with them in the morning. But you have to work, so you apologize and ask if there is another time you can get together. They get angry and tell you to forget it, and a week later you hear they split up. Now you are struggling with these feelings of guilt, even though you didn't do anything wrong!

People driven by false guilt feel they have to do everything perfectly so they don't disappoint others. I've heard it said that if false guilt were a chariot, then fear of disapproval from others is the whip upon the back of the horses pulling it. That fear can cause you to picture the worst possible scenario to your problem. It will consume your thoughts and cause you to judge yourself inaccurately and too harshly.

False guilt can also be caused by the feeling that you are responsible to save everyone that crosses your path or asks for help. Psychologists often refer to this as a savior complex. You might sacrifice your own personal needs or overextend yourself to help others because you think you are the only one who can do it.

There can be many other reasons for your false guilt, but the most likely reason is that the devil is accusing you. Revelation talks about how Satan was a fallen angel and thrown out of heaven. "This great dragon—the ancient serpent called the devil, or Satan, the one deceiving the whole world—was thrown down to the earth with all his angels. Then I heard a loud voice shouting across the heavens . . . For the *accuser* of our brothers and sisters has been thrown down to earth—the one who *accuses* them before our God day and night" (Rev. 12:9–10, emphasis mine).

The devil is a spirit and therefore has the ability to plant thoughts in your head (1 Tim. 4:1). We call it spiritual warfare because Satan always has a one-two punch. He first hits you with a temptation and then quickly hits you a second time with an accusation. Let's say he tempts you to cheat on your taxes. You dodge the first swing by resisting the temptation. But Satan then throws his second punch by whispering in your ear, "You are a terrible Christian to have thoughts of cheating on your taxes!" If you believe his lies, the guilt will eat away at you. Jesus said the devil is a liar and the father of lies. Satan doesn't want you to experience God's peace; he wants you to live under the weight of guilt.

This type of guilt is self-destructive and abusive. It will do harm to your relationship with God, with others, and with yourself. It puts a heavy burden on your back, a burden you were never intended to shoulder. Which is why Peter said, "Give all your worries and cares to God, for he cares about you" (1 Peter 5:7).

Compare the misery from false guilt to the beneficial nature of healthy guilt, or what is often referred to as godly sorrow. It's that sense of sadness you experience as a result of the sins you have committed. Paul explains it best:

> Godly sorrow brings repentance that leads to salvation and leaves no regret, but worldly sorrow brings death. See what this godly sorrow has produced in you: what earnestness, what eagerness to clear yourselves, what indignation, what alarm, what longing, what concern, what readiness to see justice done. At every point you have proved yourselves to be innocent in this matter.
>
> (2 Cor. 7:10–11 NIV)

In a Focus on the Family article, Paul Coughlin looked at the difference between healthy and harmful guilt:

> Victor Frankl . . . a Holocaust survivor . . . praised guilt as one of three components that make the case for what he called "Tragic Optimism." He said that the tragic triad of life are pain, guilt and death. Yet if handled properly, they can spur a person toward abiding meaning and purpose in life. Through guilt, he wrote, people have the potential to change for the better. Healthy guilt is a gatekeeper and boundary-maker. It helps us discover where we shouldn't go in life, what we shouldn't do. And it helps us make amends when we do cause others pain and related hardships. Guilt helps us find our way back toward what's right and repair the torn portions of our lives.[2]

In the 2 Corinthians passage we just looked at, Paul said godly sorrow leaves you with no regret. But on the other hand, false guilt leaves you with lots of regrets. *Guilt* and *regret* are two words that get tossed together a lot. They are like two brothers; they are from the same family and spend a lot of time together, but they are not the same person. In the same way guilt and regret are not exactly the same either, but it's hard to have one without the other.

And these two emotions can cause us to go down the path of "if only."

If only I had kept my mouth shut.

If only I hadn't dropped out of college.

If only I had gone with them.

"'If only' can crush hopes, steal peace, prevent forgiveness, and trap us in negative patterns of behavior. Regret is the second most frequently mentioned emotion after love."[3] Needless to say, it plays a big part in our lives.

Some people actually get so overwhelmed with guilt or regret they become physically ill, while others become so overwhelmed they take their own life. I've seen Christians walk away from their faith because they can't handle the guilt from a mistake or wrong choice they've made. Guilt is hard to live with.

Since 1811 the US Treasury department has maintained what they call a "conscience fund," where they accept repayments from Americans who feel guilty over money they believe they have defrauded the government. Most of the time the money comes back anonymously, but at times people send along a note of explanation. One person said, "Please accept the money for two postage stamps that I reused." Another wrote, "This check for $1,300 is to make restitution of tools, leave days and other things I stole while I was in the Navy from '62 to '67."[4]

I also heard it said that one man sent a check for one hundred dollars and said, "I have not been able to sleep, so here is the hundred dollars that I owe you. If I still can't sleep, I will send you the rest!"

This is what regret or guilt does: it consumes you. While the weight of it will pull you down emotionally, the disappointments will disillusion you.

If you are tired of feeling guilty all the time, why not make a decision to do something about it? Guilt is never a pleasant emotion. However, it's an emotion you can work through successfully and then, over time, eradicate from your life. So, let's look at some things we can do to overcome this habit.

Own It

The first thing you need to do is acknowledge that guilt is a problem for you. That's tough because we don't like to accept responsibility or admit we struggle with anything. "People who conceal their sins will not prosper, but if they confess and turn from them, they will receive mercy" (Prov. 28:13).

We need to come clean with God. A great example of this is found in Genesis 3. "When the cool evening breezes were blowing, the man and his wife heard the LORD God walking about in the garden. So they hid from the LORD God among the trees. Then the LORD God called to the man, 'Where are you?'" (vv. 8–9). Now I'm certain that God knew where they were hiding, but I think he wanted them to own it, to acknowledge their sin. In the same way, God wants you to acknowledge that these constant feelings of guilt are a problem for you.

There's an old story about a governor visiting one of the state prisons. He told the prisoners that he would listen to whatever they had to say. A lot of the prisoners formed a line and one by one they complained of a miscarriage of justice. "I shouldn't be here. I was framed. I didn't do the crimes they say I did." But one guy came up to the governor and said, "Sir, I'm guilty. I did the crime and I'm ashamed of my past. But the years I've been here have helped me to become a better person. And one day when I get out, I hope that I can contribute something positive to society."

The governor decided to pardon that prisoner. Why? Because he was the only one willing to accept responsibility for his behavior. Friends, that's what God will do for all who are willing to take responsibility for their sin. "Confess your sins to each other and pray for each other so that you may be healed. The earnest prayer of a righteous person has great power and produces wonderful results" (James 5:16).

Steps to a Godly Habit

STEP 1: ACCEPT GOD'S FORGIVENESS

You struggle with guilt, so you probably don't think you deserve God's forgiveness. The truth is, no one deserves God's forgiveness. It's a gift. And yet if you are not convinced that God has forgiven you, every time you have feelings of guilt you will think you deserve punishment. "I'm not a good person. I mess up all the time. I deserve God's punishment!"

That's not how God works. If you are following Christ, your past doesn't have to dictate your future because Jesus died for your guilt and regrets. The apostle Paul said, "This means that anyone who belongs to Christ has become a new person. The old life is gone; a new life has begun!" (2 Cor. 5:17). The key to overcoming regrets is being in Christ. You may want to make a fresh start or clean the slate by yourself, but you need God's help.

That's where the work of Christ takes over. John tells us, "If we confess our sins to him, he is faithful and just to forgive us our sins and to cleanse us from all wickedness" (1 John 1:9). Not only will he forgive your sins, but he will also *forget* your sins. "He has removed our sins as far from us as the east is from the west" (Ps. 103:12). He offers you a brand-new life.

If God is omniscient, or all-knowing, how can he forget our sins? It means that he puts them behind him, or in other words, he will never bring them up again. There is one thing you will never hear God say. "I remember what you did ten years ago." *No.* God said it is forgiven, and it is forgotten.

STEP 2: FORGIVE YOURSELF

Charles Stanley said, "Forgiveness is never complete until, first, we have experienced the forgiveness of God; second, we can forgive others who have wronged us; and third, we are able to forgive ourselves."[5]

To forgive yourself means to let it go, to stop beating yourself up over things that God has already forgiven and put behind him. Paul said, "No, dear brothers and sisters, I have not achieved it, but I focus on this one thing: Forgetting the past and looking forward to what lies ahead, I press on to reach the end of the race and receive the heavenly prize for which God, through Christ Jesus, is calling us" (Phil. 3:13–14). God has a purpose and plan for your life, so stop the self-punishment and start looking forward to his plan! You can torment yourself by mulling over your mistake again and again, but it's a waste of time because no amount of wallowing can change the past.

I am reminded of two disciples, Judas and Peter, who both betrayed the Lord. Judas turned Jesus over to the Pharisees for thirty pieces of silver. He struggled with so much guilt and regret that he tried to give the money back. But it still didn't get rid of his feelings of guilt, so he went out and hanged himself.

Peter, on the other hand, also betrayed the Lord. He told Jesus he was ready to go to prison or even die for him if necessary. But just a few hours later he denied even knowing Jesus. After he denied Christ the third time, a rooster crowed, and Jesus turned and looked at him. At that moment, overwhelmed with guilt and regret, Peter remembered what the Lord had said: "This very night, before the rooster crows, you will deny three times that you even know me" (Matt. 26:34). Peter left the courtyard, crying bitterly, and for several days he was left with the pain of his regret.

And yet Peter later ended up being used in a mighty way for the kingdom of God. So what was the difference between Peter and Judas? Peter owned his sin, accepted God's forgiveness, and forgave himself.

In the 1929 Rose Bowl, Georgia Tech played the University of California. Just before halftime, one of the players, Roy Riegels, recovered a fumble for California. He ran sixty-five yards—in the wrong direction. One of his own teammates tackled him at his own two-yard line. When California attempted to punt, Georgia Tech blocked it and scored a safety.

The team headed off the field and into the dressing room. Riegels sat in a corner with his face in his hands and cried like a baby. As the second half was about to begin, Coach Price said, "The same team that played the first half will start the second."

Riegels looked up with tears in his eyes and said, "Coach, I can't do it to save my life. I've ruined you, I've ruined the

University of California, I've ruined myself. I couldn't face that crowd in the stadium to save my life."

Coach Price put his hand on Roy's shoulder and said, "Roy, get up and go on back; the game is only half over." Roy got back in the game and those who were there that day said he played the greatest game of his life the second half.[6]

Like Roy Riegels, sometimes we are running in the wrong direction, or think we are running in the wrong direction, and we are not sure if we want to try anymore. Then God puts an arm around us and says, "Come on, you can do this. I will help you. The game is only half over!"

Listen, it's never too late to start over. We serve a God of second chances. Don't spend the rest of your life feeling guilty over past or perceived mistakes. I've heard it said, "Though no one can go back and make a new beginning, anyone can start from now and make a brand-new end." God has forgiven you, so you need to forgive yourself.

STEP 3: CHANGE YOUR BEHAVIOR

Instead of wasting time thinking about how terrible you are or what you should have done or not done, focus on what changes you can make in your life today, whether that's apologizing to someone or talking to someone or turning it over to God. Focus on the action items you can do to break this habit of feeling guilty.

When you start to have those feelings of guilt, ask yourself if it's deserved or if you are beating yourself up needlessly because of your own high standards. And then try to figure out what behavior or attitude you need to work on.

Maybe you need to learn to say no with a clear conscience. Maybe you've put other people's needs before your relationship with God. If so, learn to say no. They may be disappointed, and it won't feel good at first, but eventually it will create healthy boundaries in your life. And the more you establish these healthy boundaries the less you will feel guilt over trying to meet everyone's expectations. As British Reformed Baptist preacher and author Charles Spurgeon said, "Learn how to say 'no.' It will do you more good than learning Latin."[7]

Another thing you might want to consider is self-talk or encouraging yourself about dealing with this irrational guilt you feel. The guilt might have come from a parent or caretaker who constantly told you, "You can't do anything right. This is your fault. Why do you always mess up?" And now as an adult you believe those thoughts to be true, which creates feelings of guilt in most areas of your life.

But you can change that behavior by refusing to believe those lies and by reminding yourself that you are a child of God, and your guilt was crucified with Christ. He became guilty for you, for your sins, forevermore. No matter what the devil tries to accuse you of, not everything that happens is your fault. And as I said earlier, even when you make a mistake, it is forgiven and forgotten.

You can also remind yourself that the ideals you have set may simply be too high and need to be readjusted. You emotionally punish yourself with feelings of guilt because you don't think you tried hard enough when in reality it might be something that's not in you to achieve. And those incredibly high standards you judge yourself by have left you with feelings of condemnation. But Paul said, "So now there is no condemnation for those who belong to Christ Jesus" (Rom. 8:1).

STEP 4: LEARN FROM YOUR EXPERIENCES

Have you ever found yourself saying, "I'm going to stop feeling guilty about everything," only to find yourself with the same feelings of guilt a short time later? You're not alone. Habits are hard to break. But torturing yourself with feelings of false guilt will not make you a better person. And such torment is damaging to you and to the people who are close to you.

While you don't want to dwell on your past experiences with guilt, reflecting on them will help to break this bad habit once and for all. So it helps to reflect on some tough questions:

- What could I do to better handle my false guilt?
- Am I feeling guilty for something I didn't even do?
- Am I too worried about upsetting others?
- Am I always analyzing if I could have done things better?
- Am I using terms like *should have* or *could have*?
- Am I allowing something that went wrong to turn into a day of self-criticism?
- What did I learn from this?

It would be helpful if you would actually write down your responses as well as your ideas on how to respond in a healthier way. Keep your responses in a journal that you can refer back to often.

Unless you understand why you always feel guilty, it's going to be tough to make the types of changes you need to make. So learn from your past experiences so you can be the person God designed you to be.

It's now time to imagine new possibilities. But to do that you need to refocus your attention on your relationship with Christ. Only then will you experience the freedom Christ intended for you to experience. Paul said, "Christ has set us free to live a free life. So take your stand! Never again let anyone put a harness of slavery on you" (Gal. 5:1 THE MESSAGE). Just imagine how different your life will be if you don't have this weight of guilt on your shoulders.

Jesus paid for your failures and your sins; he paid for your guilt and your regrets. And the best way to silence the devil's accusations is by turning to Christ and walking in freedom.

12

PRAYERLESSNESS

The greatest tragedy of life is not
unanswered prayer, but unoffered prayer.

—F. B. Meyer

In the 1980s I was an entrepreneur and a partner in opening several businesses. One of these was a commodity trading group, which I started with my father. We would first raise a pool of money from investors and then trade it in commodities. We would buy and sell commodities such as silver, grains, even crude oil. My dad and I would sit in front of a computer screen during trading hours and watch for signals to buy or sell options in a futures contract. When you buy an option, it's risky because your dollars are leveraged, and therefore a small shift in price can cost you or make you a lot of money.

Neither one of us had been trading commodities for long, so we were not experiencing the returns we thought we would. As a result, I found myself growing more frustrated with God each day. We had already invested a lot of money into this company and felt like God had led us to open this business, and yet he didn't seem to be blessing it.

We started looking into the purchase of a computer trading system that would help us to make more profitable trades. The system that seemed to have the best track record was expensive, costing tens of thousands of dollars, so we made a trip to California to watch a live demonstration of it. It had good results, but it was going to cost a lot of money.

In the middle of this all-day demonstration, we took a break from trading and stepped outside to discuss whether we should purchase the system. We talked for a while about the positives and negatives to making such a large purchase. My dad then asked a clarifying question: "Have you been praying about this, and do you think it's God's will?" I hesitated for a moment, but then turned to him and said, "I have not been praying about it, and I don't care if it's God's will or not. We are going to buy this system!" He didn't respond, but I'm sure he was disappointed in my refusal to pray.

Even though I didn't pray about it or ask for God's wisdom, we went ahead and purchased the system. It did not perform as well as we expected. Not only did we lose a good portion of our clients' money, we lost our investment as well. We eventually closed down the company.

Prayer is our connection to God; it makes room for his direction as well as his correction. In fact, the Bible tells us to "pray continually" (1 Thess. 5:17 NIV), so anything other than a continual attitude of prayer and communion with God is disobedience. If I would have prayed about the decision to purchase that trading system, the outcome might have looked different.

In each chapter of this book I've talked about a common characteristic that, if we continue doing long enough, will form a habit in our life. I want to address prayerlessness, which at first glance might seem a bit confusing because it's not something we *do* but something we *don't* do.

Prayer is like the air we breathe; it's our lifeline, our connection to God, and it sustains us spiritually. Without prayer our spiritual life will suffocate. Without prayer we will find it difficult at best to break any of the habits that are defeating us. Which is why we need to understand how we've gotten into this habit of prayerlessness.

We have all experienced (or are experiencing) a season of prayerlessness. There are a lot of reasons why. For instance, it can be caused by misaligned priorities. You allow everything else in your life to become more important to you than time spent with God. "Certainly I believe in prayer, but I am so busy at work right now."

It can also be a stubborn independent attitude. God may be encouraging you to do something but it's not what you want to hear, so instead of listening, you stop praying.

Discouragement or resentment can be another reason for prayerlessness. Maybe you prayed for God to save your marriage and your spouse still left. Maybe you prayed for God to heal a loved one and they still died. Maybe you've been asking God for a child, but nothing has happened. And since God didn't answer your prayer, or at least not the way you wanted him to, there is a sense of betrayal and you are too hurt to pray.

There are many other reasons we won't pray, such as apathy or trusting in ourselves more than we trust in God. But whatever our reason for prayerlessness, it's essentially caused by our unbelief. *Disbelief* is to not believe God, while *unbelief* is to doubt or reject the promises of God. In Mark's gospel a man brought his demon-possessed boy to the disciples for help. They tried but were unable to help him. So the man took the boy to Jesus and said:

> "If you can do anything, take pity on us and help us."
>
> "'If you can'?" said Jesus. "Everything is possible for one who believes."
>
> Immediately the boy's father exclaimed, "I do believe; help me overcome my unbelief!"
>
> (Mark 9:22-24 NIV)

This father believed that Jesus was a healer and yet struggled to believe that he would heal his son.

Unbelief is an absence of faith. God tells us in Hebrews 11:6 that without faith it is impossible to please God. It's important to know that not only does God love us but we can also trust his promises. Because if you ignore the unbelief in your life it will lead to a backslidden condition. To be backslidden is a condition that results from spiritual apathy or disregard for the things of God. In other words, a backslider is someone moving the wrong way spiritually. Maybe at one time in their life they trusted Christ, but recently their heart has grown cold because of their unbelief. You start to notice they are no longer excited about the things of God, and you can see they are falling back into old behaviors or habits. So our unbelief is to doubt the promises of God and to question his love for us.

In an elders' meeting, Andrew Murray, a South Africa–born pastor and missionary, was asked, "What is the cause of so much prayerlessness? Is it unbelief?" He replied, "Certainly, it is unbelief, but the question is, what is the cause of the unbelief?"[1]

When you refuse to pray, there are consequences. Prayerlessness weakens your ability to hear Christ when he tries to guide and direct you, and it clouds your heart to the temptations surrounding you. That's why Jesus said, "Watch and pray so that you will not fall into temptation" (Matt. 26:41 NIV).

The Bible says in 1 Peter 1:8, "You love him even though you have never seen him. Though you do not see him now, you trust him; and you rejoice with a glorious, inexpressible joy." That inexpressible joy comes only from a right relationship with God. And you cannot have a right relationship with God if you are not spending time with him in prayer.

It also tells us in 1 Peter 5:7, "Give all your worries and cares to God, for he cares about you." How do you give your cares to God if you're not praying? A prayerless life will always lead to a more stressful life.

Another consequence of prayerlessness is that you lose any desire for more of God. Let's say you stop talking to a close friend. You will eventually lose a desire to work on that friendship. The same thing will happen if you don't ever talk to God.

Our failure to pray also demonstrates that we don't care about reaching those who are far from Christ. Because if you look back through history, you will see that most spiritual breakthroughs took place when Christians got serious about prayer. Second Chronicles 7:14 says, "If my people, who are called by my name, will humble themselves and pray . . . then I will hear from heaven . . . and will heal their land" (NIV). Prayerlessness limits what God will do in our world.

I want you to understand that prayerlessness is sin. In his epistle, James said, "It is sin to know what you ought to do and then not do it" (4:17). The definition of sin is to miss the mark. In the book of Romans it says that "whatever is not from faith is sin" (14:23 NKJV). Sin is any lack of conformity to the moral character of God. We sin with our evil thoughts, or when we speak evil, act evil, or fail to do good. Sin is anything that stands between us and God. And a prayerless life makes no room for God. It was John Bunyan who said, "Prayer will make a man cease from sin, or sin will entice a man to cease from prayer."[2]

There are two types of sin: sins of commission, which are actions we commit, and sins of omission, which are things we should have done but failed to do. Therefore, prayerlessness is a lack of action and would be considered a sin of omission.

The prophet Samuel clearly viewed prayerlessness as sin. When he confronted the people of Israel with their sin, they recognized he was right and asked him for his prayers. Listen to his response: "As for me, far be it from me that I should sin against the LORD by failing to pray for you" (1 Sam. 12:23 NIV).

Billy Graham warned of the dangers of prayerlessness: "We are to pray in times of adversity, lest we become faithless and unbelieving. We are to pray in times of prosperity, lest we become boastful and proud. We are to pray in times of danger, lest we become fearful and doubting. We are to pray in times of security, lest we become self-sufficient."[3]

James told us, "A prayer of a righteous person, when it is brought about, can accomplish much" (James 5:16 NASB). If that's true, then it makes sense that prayerlessness is why so many believers seem weak and ineffective. Or why there seems to be so much effort in the church at times with so little results. We say we want to be led by the Spirit, but prayerlessness leaves us walking in the flesh. Prayerlessness is to settle for less than God's best.

I heard a story of a pastor who asked his church to pray that

God would shut down the neighborhood bar. The entire church gathered for a prayer meeting asking God to rid the neighborhood of it. A few weeks later lightning struck the bar, and it burned to the ground. The owner of the bar heard about this prayer meeting and decided to bring a lawsuit against the church. As they stood in front of the judge that day, the owner argued that God struck his bar with lightning because of the prayers of this church. The pastor admitted they did indeed have a prayer meeting for that purpose, but no one in his congregation really expected anything to happen. The judge then leaned back in his chair and just shook his head. He said, "I can't believe what I am hearing. I have a bar owner who believes in the power of prayer and a pastor who doesn't!"

There are a lot of Christians who say they believe in the importance of prayer, and yet their actions show otherwise. On the other hand, there are a lot of Christians who want to pray but just don't know how. The disciples were so discouraged by their own lack of prayer that they asked Jesus to teach them to pray. Out of all the things they could have asked him for, why prayer? Because they saw how effective it was in Jesus' life. They watched him turn water into wine and give sight to the blind. They were there when he fed the five thousand and raised the dead. And yet they didn't ask him how to teach, or how to forgive, or how to do miracles. They wanted to learn how to be effective in their prayers.

There is nothing more important to the effectiveness of your Christian life than prayer. Everything within us wants to follow our own selfish ambitions and the lure of this world. But prayer is what keeps us centered and focused on God. Prayer is an act of obedience and dedication to the Lord. Prayer is what drowns out the noise and confusion of the world. Prayer is our lifeline or our communication with God.

Communication is the basis of life. Whenever there's healthy communication there is a healthy relationship, but when there's no communication you have a broken relationship. The Cuban Missile Crisis in 1962 was basically a standoff between President Kennedy and Premier Khrushchev of the Soviet Union. It was a moment when the two superpowers came close to an all-out nuclear war over the planting of missiles in Cuba. One of the outcomes of that near encounter was the establishment of a direct communication link between the United States and the Soviet Union, known as the hotline agreement. To help speed up and enhance communication, there would now be a direct line on the desk of the president of the United States as well as the desk of the premier of the Soviet Union.

We need to be reminded that communication is always the key to any healthy relationship. What an incredible privilege we have been given to communicate with the God of the universe. And yet until we realize how desperately we need him, we won't pray. The greatest tragedy in life is the prayers that go unanswered because they go unasked. Let's take a look at what you can do to overcome prayerlessness in your life.

Own It

You are certainly not the first person to struggle with prayerlessness. We have all experienced it at one time or another. We know the disciples of Jesus struggled with prayer. Which is why they once asked him to teach them how to pray. They had observed his life and saw that his prayers were effective, so they wanted to create this habit of prayer in their lives as well.

Without prayer, your relationship with Christ will not be healthy. You will come up with 101 excuses why you don't have time to pray. And even when you do make an attempt to pray it will be hard to focus, your mind will wander, and it will feel like your words are not even making it through the ceiling.

So the question is, What steps do you need to take to stop this habit of prayerlessness? The first thing is to acknowledge that your lack of prayer is sin. And then once you have confessed it to God, ask him for the motivation to change. You should never be content to sit in a season of prayerlessness but rather acknowledge that you are in one and labor to remedy it.

Steps to a Godly Habit

STEP 1: IDENTIFY YOUR OBSTACLES

There can be many things that keep us from prayer. But it's important to identify what those obstacles are in your life. For instance, do you have a hard time concentrating when you pray? Where does your mind drift off to? Because whatever that is, is likely an obstacle.

Are there things that upset you so much you can't pray about them? Maybe a strained relationship or unresolved conflict? In the Sermon on the Mount Jesus said, "If you are presenting a sacrifice at the altar in the Temple and you suddenly remember that someone has something against you, leave your sacrifice there at the altar. Go and be reconciled to that person. Then come and offer your sacrifice to God" (Matt. 5:23–24). Your prayers will never be effective until you resolve that conflict in your life. God wants us to be in unity with one another.

Or what about the motivation of your heart when it comes to prayer? In other words, do you only pray because of your own self-gratification? Are you only praying because you want to impress others with how spiritual you are? Why are you praying? James said, "You ask and do not receive, because you ask with wrong motives, so that you may spend what you request on your pleasures" (James 4:3 NASB). Make sure your motives don't become an obstacle in your communication with God.

Is there unforgiveness in your life? Because if there is, it will contaminate your heart and your prayers. The prophet Isaiah wrote, "It's your sins that have cut you off from God. Because of your sins, he has turned away and will not listen anymore" (59:2). If, every time I pray, the Holy Spirit convicts me of my unforgiveness, I will either deal with the unforgiveness or I will stop praying. And if I want the Spirit's guidance in my life, then forgiving others is critical.

Once you get your obstacles out of the way, it will become much easier to break the cycle of prayerlessness.

STEP 2: SCHEDULE A TIME TO PRAY

A lot of Christians don't feel like they pray enough. And if prayerlessness is a sin, then how much do we need to pray to satisfy God? The problem with this question is that it indicates your heart is either not right or you don't understand the reason for prayer. It would be like me asking, "How much do I need to talk to my wife each day to satisfy her?" That's a wrong perspective. The reality is I love her, so I want to spend time with her. I want to talk to her, and I want her to talk to me. How else can I get to know her and develop my relationship with her?

The same should be true in your relationship with God. You should want to spend time with God because you love him. Paul wrote in Philippians 3:10, "I want to know Christ and experience the mighty power that raised him from the dead." If you really want to know the heart of your God, then spend time with him, communicate with him, and listen for that still, small voice as he communicates with you.

Oftentimes we want someone to give us a formula. "If you pray for ten minutes each day, you will be okay." The problem is that someone else will come along and say, "You need to pray for one hour a day." And then someone else will weigh in, and on and on it will go. Prayer is not measured by the minutes or the hours, so don't worry about some man-made rules or requirements.

The secret sauce to a successful prayer life is having a dedicated time each day to get alone with God. During the day I find it easy to keep the communication lines open and ongoing with God. I will talk to him while I'm driving my car or while I'm trying to make a decision. It's almost like multitasking, but I do it to keep my thoughts focused on him.

But because my life is so busy it's harder to have a scheduled time with him. I have to be intentional to make it happen. Again, it's similar to my marriage. Sandy and I talk while we are doing other things, but if we want a strong marriage, we know we have to schedule time to set everything else aside and talk. That's what I need to do with God. Whether that's for ten minutes or two hours, I need to set aside that daily time with God. And I do think you'll find the more time you spend with God, the closer you will get to him, and the more you will look forward to that daily time with him.

STEP 3: FIND A PRAYER PARTNER

Finding someone of the same sex to pray with on a regular basis can help you have the accountability you need to stick with it and break the habit of prayerlessness. That is why Jesus encourages us to pray together. "If two of you agree here on earth concerning anything you ask, my Father in heaven will do it for you" (Matt. 18:19). There is so much good that can come from two people praying together.

Prayer isn't meant to be self-centered. When you pray with someone else your prayers are no longer all about you. Having a prayer partner will help you to focus on each other's needs as well as the needs of others. There might be times you are going through a difficult struggle and just don't have the words to pray. Having someone who cares about you pray on your behalf is a wonderful experience, and hearing them pray for your situation will also help you to refocus on Christ. When I know someone is praying for me and agreeing with me in prayer, it is such an encouragement. I've always loved this passage:

> Two people are better off than one, for they can help each other succeed. If one person falls, the other can reach out and help. But someone who falls alone is in real trouble. Likewise, two people lying close together can keep each other warm. But how can one be warm alone? A person standing alone can be attacked and defeated, but two can stand back-to-back and conquer. Three are even better, for a triple-braided cord is not easily broken.
>
> (Eccl. 4:9–12)

And whether you come together with your prayer partner in person or on the phone, it should be someone whom you trust, someone who is growing in their faith. Because you will want to be open and honest with each other and share the good, the bad, and the ugly. However, it's also important that you don't mistake your time together as a counseling session or an opportunity to unload all your gripes and complaints. Doing that will miss the point of praying together. Stay focused on prayer.

STEP 4: USE AN OUTLINE

Creating a habit of prayer can be difficult for all of us. I can become easily distracted when it comes to my time in prayer. My mind tends to drift away from the things I'm praying for to the things I need to get done. So I've found it is helpful to use a prayer formula or outline to keep me focused. It also reminds me to pray for things I might have otherwise failed to include.

Sometimes it helps to write out your prayers in a journal. Other times it helps to pray Scripture. Think of it as a dialogue: God speaks to you through his Word and prayer is our response. And if you pray through Scripture you will never run out of things to pray about.

There are a lot of good formulas or outlines you can use, so I don't think it matters which one you pick. Just select one and try it for several days. Regardless of which one you use, just make sure you allow time to listen to God. Here are a few examples of the more common ones.

The first example, the five-finger prayer, uses the fingers on your hand as a roadmap.

Thumb—Pray for the people you love.

Index finger (pointing finger)—Pray for those who teach: teachers, clergy, counselors.

Middle finger (tallest one)—Pray for those who are in authority over you: national and local leaders, employers, and first responders such as police and firefighters.

Ring finger (your weakest finger)—Pray for those who are weak or hurting: children, the poor, sick, and homeless.

Pinky finger (your smallest finger)—Pray for your own needs, as this one reminds you of your smallness compared to God.

Think about taking a TRIP with God, which can be a useful acrostic. Ask yourself the following questions:

T—Thanks: What am I thankful for?
R—Regret: What are the things that I regret?
I—Intercession: Whom do I need to intercede for?
P—Purpose: What is God's purpose or plan for my life?

Another common acrostic that's helpful is the PARTS of prayer:

P—Praise
A—Ask
R—Repent
T—Thank
S—Share

Perhaps the most well-known acrostic prayer is ACTS:

A—Adoration: Praise God for who he is.
C—Confession: Own up to your sins.
T—Thanksgiving: Thank God for all he has done.
S—Supplication: Make requests for yourself and others.

The model that I have used most of my adult life is the Lord's Prayer. Many believe, as I do, that Jesus intended for it to be an outline that would help guide our prayer time. The idea is that there are five sections and you pray through each. Whether you use it to pray for five minutes a day or fifty minutes a day, it will help you to stay focused and on track.

Adoration

In Matthew 6 Jesus said to the disciples, "This, then, is how you should pray." He started by saying, "Our Father in heaven, hallowed be your name" (v. 9 NIV). That's adoration or worship. In other words, you don't start with making requests. You start with giving God the worship and praise he deserves, which helps to focus you on Jesus and how amazing he is.

Consecration

After you have worshiped you move to "Your kingdom come, your will be done" (v. 10 NIV). This is consecration, which means to surrender or to set yourself apart to be used by God. You are asking God to establish his kingdom in your life as well as in the community. You are also praying that his plan and purpose will be accomplished in your life. In other words, I don't want my life to be driven by my own independent spirit. I want God's will for my life. This section is really more of a declaration that you are aligning your heart with God's.

Supplication

The next section is "Give us today our daily bread" (v. 11 NIV). This is supplication, so I'm now ready to ask God for specific needs. In other words, make a list of the things you need in your life and call out each in prayer.

Intercession

The next section of the prayer is "Forgive us our debts as we also have forgiven our debtors" (v. 12 NIV). This is intercession. It's doing just what it says to do: asking God to forgive you for the things you've done wrong and to help you to forgive all of those who have done you wrong. It's hard to stay angry at someone you are asking God to forgive.

Deliverance

The next section says, "Lead us not into temptation, but deliver us from the evil one" (v. 13 NIV). This is praying for protection from the lies and attacks of the enemy. We need to recognize that Satan is a liar and will do everything he can to try and tempt us. Scripture says, "We are not fighting against flesh-and-blood enemies, but against evil rulers and authorities of the unseen world, against mighty powers in this dark world, and against evil spirits in the heavenly places" (Eph. 6:12). Which is why we need to pray for God to give us the discernment and wisdom to not give in to temptation.

Find a model or outline and give it a try for a couple of weeks and see if it resonates with you. If it doesn't just try another until you find one that helps you to grow in this habit of prayer.

STEP 5: PRAY WITH BOLDNESS

I once heard a pastor say that God does not answer vague prayers. I'm not sure if that's true, but I do know that God wants us to be bold with our prayers. You don't have to look far in Scripture to find numerous examples of people praying bold prayers. Think about Moses standing in front of the Red Sea asking God to deliver the Israelites from the Egyptian army. Or what about when Joshua prayed that God would help the Israelites in their battle by stopping the sun. Or Elijah when he prayed for God to send fire down from heaven and consume the altar.

But I think one of my favorite examples of bold prayers is that of the mother of James and John. "Then the mother of James and John, the sons of Zebedee, came to Jesus with her sons. She knelt respectfully to ask a favor. 'What is your request?' he asked. She replied, 'In your Kingdom, please let my two sons sit in places of honor next to you, one on your right and the other on your left'" (Matt. 20:20–21).

This mother didn't ask if her sons could one day hold the door for Jesus; she wanted her boys to be on the right and left sides of Jesus in heaven. Now that's a bold prayer. Many think she stepped over the line. I don't think she did. What loving mother hasn't gone the extra mile in trying to achieve what's best for her kids?

God may or may not answer your prayers in the way you want, but Scripture tells us that bold prayers are exactly what the Lord wants from us. That's why Jesus said, "Keep on asking, and you will receive what you ask for. Keep on seeking, and you will find. Keep on knocking, and the door will be opened to you. For everyone who asks, receives. Everyone who seeks, finds. And to everyone who knocks, the door will be opened" (Matt. 7:7–8).

God doesn't want us to be shy when it comes to the things of God. The book of James tells us, "You don't have what you want because you don't ask God for it" (4:2). If you have a need, then be bold enough to take it to God! Billy Graham once said, "This should be the motto of every follower of Jesus Christ. No matter how dark and hopeless a situation might seem, never stop praying."[4]

I'm not saying that bold prayers are the only way we communicate with God. Sometimes we need to be still and listen for that still, small voice; we need to contemplate what the Spirit of God is saying to us. I'm just saying that it's important for us to push through passivity and apathy and put ourselves in alignment with God. When you believe that God loves you and is for you, you will pray bold prayers. If not, your prayers will be timid and laced with skepticism. So always remember that bold prayers honor God and God honors bold prayers.

The Bible is clear that we have an obligation to pray. But maintaining an effective prayer life requires ongoing effort. If you want prayer to be a way of life, then the only thing left to do is practice praying. Not just when you are in a crisis mode but every day of your life. Just decide you are going to do it. What if someone told you that if you didn't take a certain medication every single night before midnight, you would be dead the next day. You would absolutely make sure you took those meds. Prayer is that important. That's why it's vital that you make a place for prayer in your daily routine. There are two phrases that have always helped me, and I hope you will always remember them as well. "A prayerless Christian is a powerless Christian," and "Where prayer focuses, power falls."

EPILOGUE

A change in bad habits leads
to a change in life.

—Jenny Craig

We are creatures of habit, and those habits can have a powerful hold on our lives. There is an old Spanish proverb that says, "Habits begin like threads in a spider's web, but end like the chains in a prison." There are few things that will have a greater impact on your life than cooperating with the Holy Spirit to improve your daily habits. I have often heard it said that we first make our habits, and then our habits make us.

The police department in the Philippines hired a steel worker named Mang Karin to build a cage to hold people after they were arrested. Once Karin had finished the cage and was paid, he went out with friends and drank all night. Drunk and staggering home, he was picked up by the police for violating curfew. They took him to the police station and put him in a steel cage—the very one he had just built.[1]

You might ignore your bad habit because you think it's no more than an annoyance. But when you ignore that habit long enough, it will become a stronghold in your life. In Scripture Paul used the term *stronghold* to describe a mindset or an attitude. It's like you've built your own cage and now the devil is using it to hold you captive. Dr. Samuel Johnson, the compiler of the first English dictionary, said, "Habits are chains that are too small to be felt until they are too strong to be broken."[2]

Do you have a bad habit that has become a stronghold in your life?

- Pride
- Anger
- Excuses
- Lust
- Cynicism
- Worry
- Complaining
- Workaholism
- Lying
- Idolatry
- Guilt
- Prayerlessness

You can't just grit your teeth and try harder to defeat a stronghold. You don't have the power to pull this off on your own—you need God's help. Paul said our weapons are from God and they have divine power to demolish the stronghold in our life.

> For though we live in the world, we do not wage war as the world does. The weapons we fight with are not the weapons of the world. On the contrary, they have divine power to

> demolish strongholds. We demolish arguments and every pretension that sets itself up against the knowledge of God, and we take captive every thought to make it obedient to Christ. And we will be ready to punish every act of disobedience, once your obedience is complete.
>
> (2 Cor. 10:3–6 NIV)

And yet once you've taken the steps to break a habit in your life, it's easy to get sidetracked. It stops being a priority, so you become complacent; you stop praying about it; you stop working on it. You know you haven't really finished dealing with it, but you've improved just enough that it doesn't feel as pressing as it used to. You begin to rationalize old patterns. "I don't think my habit was really all that bad anyway."

That's when it's good to have an accountability partner, someone who will come alongside and encourage you. Listen, with God's help you can do this on your own, but you will find it much easier with the support of a friend. Trying to break these old habits without support is like driving a car seventy miles per hour and taking your hands off the steering wheel. You may not crash right away but it's going to be very difficult to avoid.

Another thing that can cause you to get sidetracked is to ignore the steps. We live in a microwave society that wants everything right now. We want all of our bad habits gone today. And yet your habit was not created overnight, and it will not go away overnight either. God is at work in your life, but you need to remember it's a process.

I would encourage you to daily evaluate how you are doing on replacing these habits. Spend time alone with God first thing in the morning or before you go to bed at night. Meditate on the Word of God or on the whispers of the Holy Spirit. To meditate is to ponder or reflect on what God is saying to you concerning these habits. And don't give up!

If you are familiar with Tony Horton and his intense exercise routine P90X, you know he is trying to help people replace some of their bad habits with healthy exercise and nutrition. The program is comprised of six one-hour sessions per week for ninety days. Tony Horton encourages his devotees with the line "keep pressing play." In other words, on those days when you are tired and your muscles hurt and you think you have better things to do, keep pressing Play. On those days you just don't want to do the work, when you would rather stay in bed, keep pressing Play. Today you might only accomplish ten minutes of a one-hour workout. That's okay. Just get up tomorrow and hit Play.

That's great advice. It's important to create good habits when it comes to taking care of our bodies. Paul said, "Do not waste time arguing over godless ideas and old wives' tales. Instead, train yourself to be godly. 'Physical training is good, but training for godliness is much better, promising benefits in this life and in the life to come'" (1 Tim. 4:7–8). How do you train yourself to godliness? By daily making a decision to practice righteousness. When you do that you are forming new habits. It doesn't matter what mistakes you might have made yesterday. Today you keep pressing Play and put yesterday's disappointments behind you as you look forward to a new opportunity, a fresh start, a clean slate.

As we come to the end of this book, I hope you have figured out which habit you want to work on first. If it's a topic in this book, I would go back and read that chapter again. Mark Twain once said, "The secret of getting ahead is getting started. The secret of getting started is breaking your complex overwhelming tasks into small manageable tasks, and starting on the first one."[3]

And yet total freedom will not come from reading one book. It will come when you decide you are ready to make a change. The steps I've talked about in this book can take months to process and live out. Therefore, to experience lasting freedom, you will need to move from a one-time attempt to a change of lifestyle. In other words, the goal is to permanently build these healthy habits into your life.

Listen, my friends, God loves you more than you can ever begin to imagine, and he wants to see you eliminate these destructive and sinful habits from your life. But you have to decide if you are ready to break the cycle of bad habits and replace them with good ones, with spiritual disciplines that will further your spiritual growth. And if you are, then ask God for his help. Because apart from him you have little chance of defeating these bad habits. You might have some success on your own, but with his help your success will be amplified.

I love the Serenity Prayer used by Alcoholics Anonymous: "God, grant me the serenity to accept the things I cannot change, courage to change the things I can, and wisdom to know the difference." Choose which habit you want to eliminate, ask God for his help, and keep pressing Play!

The content of this book is based on sermons I preached, which are now available at www.StevePoeMinistries.com/Resources. I welcome your thoughts at info@StevePoeMinistries.com.

QUESTIONS FOR REFLECTION

Chapter 1: Pride

1. What are ways pride has been a good thing in your life? What are ways pride has been a problem for you?
2. Why did C. S. Lewis call pride "the Great Sin"?
3. Give several examples of how self-centered pride is at the very heart of our sinful nature.
4. Can you think of ways that a self-centered, prideful person would know that pride is becoming a habit?
5. How has your self-centered pride kept you from God's purpose being accomplished in your life?
6. If humility is the antidote to pride, what can we do to grow humility in our lives?
7. Who is one of the humblest people you know? What are some of the characteristics that you admire about them?

GOING DEEPER

The Lord detests the proud;
    they will surely be punished.
Pride goes before destruction,
    and haughtiness before a fall.
Better to live humbly with the poor
    than to share plunder with the proud.

(Prov. 16:5, 18–19)

You should know this, Timothy, that in the last days there will be very difficult times. For people will love only themselves and their money. They will be boastful and proud, scoffing at God, disobedient to their parents, and ungrateful. They will consider nothing sacred.

(2 Tim. 3:1–2)

Those who belong to Christ Jesus have nailed the passions and desires of their sinful nature to his cross and crucified them there. Since we are living by the Spirit, let us follow the Spirit's leading in every part of our lives. Let us not become conceited, or provoke one another, or be jealous of one another.

(Gal. 5:24–26)

Chapter 2: Anger

1. Can you think of a time you lost your temper? How did it make you feel later?

2. If anger is a God-given emotion, then how can it be expressed in a healthy way?
3. If anger is a secondary emotion, what are the things in your life that bring on anger for you?
4. What are some steps you can take to manage or control your anger?
5. Was there a lot of anger in your home growing up? How did it affect you?
6. Do you use yelling to motivate people? How does it affect your relationships?
7. Why does an unhealthy expression of anger alienate people and damage relationships?
8. What are things you do to calm down when you feel anger rising up in you?

GOING DEEPER

> And "don't sin by letting anger control you." Don't let the sun go down while you are still angry, for anger gives a foothold to the devil. If you are a thief, quit stealing. Instead, use your hands for good hard work, and then give generously to others in need. Don't use foul or abusive language. Let everything you say be good and helpful, so that your words will be an encouragement to those who hear them. And do not bring sorrow to God's Holy Spirit by the way you live. Remember, he has identified you as his own, guaranteeing that you will be saved on the day of redemption. Get rid of all bitterness, rage, anger, harsh words, and slander, as well as all types of evil behavior.
>
> (Eph. 4:26–31)

Stop being angry!
  Turn from your rage!
Do not lose your temper—
  it only leads to harm.
For the wicked will be destroyed,
  but those who trust in the Lord will possess the land.

(Ps. 37:8–9)

Control your temper,
  for anger labels you a fool.

(Eccl. 7:9)

Don't befriend angry people
  or associate with hot-tempered people.

(Prov. 22:24)

Chapter 3: Excuses

1. What is the funniest or most outrageous excuse you have ever heard someone make?
2. Think of an example where you made an excuse that derailed your dream. How were you able to correct it?
3. Can you think of a time someone let you down and then made a lame excuse to try and justify what they did? How did that make you feel? How did it affect your relationship with them?
4. What are some excuses we use for not serving God?
5. Philippians 4:13 shows us that what we cannot do in our own strength, God can. Pray together for your family, or

as a group pray that God would help you stop making excuses so you can do the things he has called you to do.

GOING DEEPER

Hearing this, a man sitting at the table with Jesus exclaimed, "What a blessing it will be to attend a banquet in the Kingdom of God!"

Jesus replied with this story: "A man prepared a great feast and sent out many invitations. When the banquet was ready, he sent his servant to tell the guests, 'Come, the banquet is ready.' But they all began making excuses. One said, 'I have just bought a field and must inspect it. Please excuse me.' Another said, 'I have just bought five pairs of oxen, and I want to try them out. Please excuse me.' Another said, 'I just got married, so I can't come.'

"The servant returned and told his master what they had said. His master was furious and said, 'Go quickly into the streets and alleys of the town and invite the poor, the crippled, the blind, and the lame.' After the servant had done this, he reported, 'There is still room for more.' So his master said, 'Go out into the country lanes and behind the hedges and urge anyone you find to come, so that the house will be full. For none of those I first invited will get even the smallest taste of my banquet.'"

(LUKE 14:15–24)

"And why worry about a speck in your friend's eye when you have a log in your own? How can you think of saying to your friend, 'Let me help you get rid of that speck in your eye,' when you can't see past the log in your own eye? Hypocrite! First get rid of the log in your own eye; then you will see well enough to deal with the speck in your friend's eye."

(MATT. 7:3–5)

Chapter 4: Lust

1. What steps would you be willing to take to remove the temptations of lust from your life?
2. How do you hold yourself accountable when it comes to the sin of lust?
3. Where do you feel you are most vulnerable to lust?
4. How would you describe the difference between lust and love?
5. How can lust hurt your marriage?
6. How does lust lie to us? What cost does lust carry?

GOING DEEPER

In the spring, at the time when kings go off to war, David sent Joab out with the king's men and the whole Israelite army. They destroyed the Ammonites and besieged Rabbah. But David remained in Jerusalem.

One evening David got up from his bed and walked around on the roof of the palace. From the roof he saw a woman bathing. The woman was very beautiful, and David sent someone to find out about her. The man said, "She is Bathsheba, the daughter of Eliam and the wife of Uriah the Hittite." Then David sent messengers to get her. She came to him, and he slept with her. (Now she was purifying herself from her monthly uncleanness.) Then she went back home. The woman conceived and sent word to David, saying, "I am pregnant."

(2 Sam. 11:1–5 NIV)

Drink water from your own cistern,
running water from your own well.
Should your springs overflow in the streets,
your streams of water in the public squares?
Let them be yours alone,
never to be shared with strangers.
May your fountain be blessed,
and may you rejoice in the wife of your youth.
A loving doe, a graceful deer—
may her breasts satisfy you always,
may you ever be intoxicated with her love.
Why, my son, be intoxicated with another man's wife?
Why embrace the bosom of a wayward woman?
For your ways are in full view of the Lord,
and he examines all your paths.
The evil deeds of the wicked ensnare them;
the cords of their sins hold them fast.
For lack of discipline they will die,
led astray by their own great folly.

(Prov. 5:15–23 NIV)

Chapter 5: Cynicism

1. Are you cynical? Can you give examples of times you have been cynical?
2. How is cynicism affecting your relationships? Do you have someone in your life who is cynical?
3. Do you find it hard to trust people?

4. Can you think of something in your childhood that has caused you to be cynical as an adult?
5. Adopting a curious, hopeful outlook on life can keep you from becoming cynical. What are some specific ways you can create and cultivate a more hopeful perspective?
6. Why are we less cynical as children than we are as adults?
7. The irony of cynicism is that it doesn't happen because you don't care; it happens because you do care. How has that been true in your life?

GOING DEEPER

Then they said to Moses, "Is it because there were no graves in Egypt that you have taken us away to die in the wilderness? Why have you dealt with us in this way, bringing us out of Egypt? Is this not the word that we spoke to you in Egypt, saying, 'Leave us alone that we may serve the Egyptians'? For it would have been better for us to serve the Egyptians than to die in the wilderness!"

(Ex. 14:11–12 NASB)

"Beware of your friends;
do not trust anyone in your clan.
For every one of them is a deceiver,
and every friend a slanderer.
Friend deceives friend,
and no one speaks the truth.
They have taught their tongues to lie;
they weary themselves with sinning.
You live in the midst of deception;
in their deceit they refuse to acknowledge me."

(Jer. 9:4–6 NIV)

And so they watched Him, and sent spies who pretended to be righteous, in order that they might catch Him in some statement, so that they could hand Him over to the jurisdiction and authority of the governor. And the spies questioned Him, saying, "Teacher, we know that You speak and teach correctly, and You are not partial to anyone, but You teach the way of God on the basis of truth. Is it permissible for us to pay taxes to Caesar, or not?" But He saw through their trickery and said to them, "Show Me a denarius. Whose image and inscription does it have?" They said, "Caesar's." And He said to them, "Then pay to Caesar the things that are Caesar's, and to God the things that are God's." And they were unable to catch Him in a statement in the presence of the people; and they were amazed at His answer, and said nothing.

(LUKE 20:20–26 NASB)

Chapter 6: Worry

1. Do you worry too much? What is the silliest thing you've ever worried about?
2. Why do you think we worry so much, even though we know God will take care of us?
3. Why does God want to take on our problems?
4. Do you ever hear people try to rationalize their worry? What are some of the reasons they use to justify their worry?
5. What triggers worry in your life?
6. How do you think unhealthy lifestyle choices make you more prone to worry?

GOING DEEPER

As Jesus and the disciples continued on their way to Jerusalem, they came to a certain village where a woman named Martha welcomed him into her home. Her sister, Mary, sat at the Lord's feet, listening to what he taught. But Martha was distracted by the big dinner she was preparing. She came to Jesus and said, "Lord, doesn't it seem unfair to you that my sister just sits here while I do all the work? Tell her to come and help me."

But the Lord said to her, "My dear Martha, you are worried and upset over all these details! There is only one thing worth being concerned about. Mary has discovered it, and it will not be taken away from her."

(Luke 10:38–42)

Then Jesus said, "Come to me, all of you who are weary and carry heavy burdens, and I will give you rest. Take my yoke upon you. Let me teach you, because I am humble and gentle at heart, and you will find rest for your souls. For my yoke is easy to bear, and the burden I give you is light."

(Matt. 11:28–30)

So refuse to worry, and keep your body healthy. But remember that youth, with a whole life before you, is meaningless.

(Eccl. 11:10)

Chapter 7: Complaining

1. What kinds of things do you find yourself complaining about?
2. What happens when you encounter a person who complains about everything? How does it make you feel and how do you usually respond?
3. When it comes to our jobs, our families, and our friendships, what is the overall "cost" of complaining?
4. What is your complaining style—polite or aggressive?
5. Take another look at the six steps to break the habit of complaining and decide which you need to focus on the most:

   Step 1: Undergo a complaint detox
   Step 2: Practice being positive
   Step 3: Practice expressing gratitude
   Step 4: Practice being content
   Step 5: Be less judgmental
   Step 6: Bite your tongue

GOING DEEPER

Let everything you say be good and helpful, so that your words will be an encouragement to those who hear them.

(EPH. 4:29)

A good person produces good things from the treasury of a good heart, and an evil person produces evil things from the treasury of an evil heart. What you say flows from what is in your heart.

(LUKE 6:45)

Do not grumble against one another, brothers, so that you may not be judged; behold, the Judge is standing at the door.

(James 5:9 ESV)

Let no corrupting talk come out of your mouths, but only such as is good for building up, as fits the occasion, that it may give grace to those who hear.

(Eph. 4:29 ESV)

Chapter 8: Workaholism

1. Do you get more excited about your work than you do about family events?
2. How would you describe the differences between a hard worker and a workaholic?
3. Do you think about your work while in the car, while falling asleep at night, or even while others are talking?
4. How can you adjust your schedule to create more rest and family time?
5. Do you work on your phone or read while you are at dinner with your family?
6. Have your family and friends given up expecting you to arrive on time?
7. What are ways workaholism is offensive to your relationship with God?

GOING DEEPER

Unless the Lord builds a house,
    the work of the builders is wasted.
Unless the Lord protects a city,
    guarding it with sentries will do no good.
It is useless for you to work so hard
    from early morning until late at night,
anxiously working for food to eat;
    for God gives rest to his loved ones.

(Ps. 127:1–2)

Don't store up treasures here on earth, where moths eat them and rust destroys them, and where thieves break in and steal. Store your treasures in heaven, where moths and rust cannot destroy, and thieves do not break in and steal. Wherever your treasure is, there the desires of your heart will also be.

(Matt. 6:19–21)

Chapter 9: Lying

1. What areas of lying do you need to work on avoiding?
2. Can you remember a time you were caught in a lie?
3. Have you ever been hurt by someone's lies?
4. Are there ever good reasons for lying? Give examples of what you think are harmless white lies.
5. Did you ever lie to your parents and get away with it?
6. What do you think it means to tame the tongue?
7. What steps have you taken to be a person of integrity?

GOING DEEPER

An honest witness does not lie;
a false witness breathes lies.

(PROV. 14:5)

Then Peter said, "Ananias, why have you let Satan fill your heart? You lied to the Holy Spirit, and you kept some of the money for yourself. The property was yours to sell or not sell, as you wished. And after selling it, the money was also yours to give away. How could you do a thing like this? You weren't lying to us but to God!"

As soon as Ananias heard these words, he fell to the floor and died. Everyone who heard about it was terrified. Then some young men got up, wrapped him in a sheet, and took him out and buried him.

(ACTS 5:3–6)

Don't lie to each other, for you have stripped off your old sinful nature and all its wicked deeds.

(COL. 3:9)

Outside the city are the dogs—the sorcerers, the sexually immoral, the murderers, the idol worshipers, and all who love to live a lie.

(REV. 22:15)

Chapter 10: Idolatry

1. After reading this chapter, do you think you have been practicing idolatry without realizing it?
2. When you think of an idol in your life, what is the first thing that comes to your mind?
3. How do you respond when your idols are threatened or taken away (anger, fear, etc.)?
4. What obstacles seem to keep you from what you crave or want? Is it possible that God put the obstacle in front of you to keep you from that idol?
5. God is a jealous God. What does that mean and how does it impact our understanding of him?
6. Finish these sentences:

    Life only has meaning if ____________.

    All I ever wanted is ________________.

    Could it be your answers indicate an idol in your life?
7. If idols are the things that capture your imagination, then what do you daydream about?
8. If the way out of idolatry is to turn back to the living God, what are actions you could take?

GOING DEEPER

Be very careful never to make a treaty with the people who live in the land where you are going. If you do, you will follow their evil ways and be trapped. Instead, you must break down their pagan altars, smash their sacred pillars, and cut down their Asherah poles. You must worship no other gods, for the LORD, whose very name is Jealous, is a God who is jealous about his relationship with you.

(EX. 34:12–14)

You adulterers! Don't you realize that friendship with the world makes you an enemy of God? I say it again: If you want to be a friend of the world, you make yourself an enemy of God. Do you think the Scriptures have no meaning? They say that God is passionate that the spirit he has placed within us should be faithful to him.

(James 4:4–5)

Then Nebuchadnezzar flew into a rage and ordered that Shadrach, Meshach, and Abednego be brought before him. When they were brought in, Nebuchadnezzar said to them, "Is it true, Shadrach, Meshach, and Abednego, that you refuse to serve my gods or to worship the gold statue I have set up? I will give you one more chance to bow down and worship the statue I have made when you hear the sound of the musical instruments. But if you refuse, you will be thrown immediately into the blazing furnace. And then what god will be able to rescue you from my power?"

Shadrach, Meshach, and Abednego replied, "O Nebuchadnezzar, we do not need to defend ourselves before you. If we are thrown into the blazing furnace, the God whom we serve is able to save us. He will rescue us from your power, Your Majesty. But even if he doesn't, we want to make it clear to you, Your Majesty, that we will never serve your gods or worship the gold statue you have set up."

(Dan. 3:13–18)

Chapter 11: Guilt

1. Can you give an example of a time you felt healthy guilt or godly sorrow?
2. Can you give examples of false guilt you have struggled with?
3. Read 1 Timothy 1:15. How does Christ's forgiveness of Paul help you in your situation?
4. In what areas are you unnecessarily blaming yourself?
5. What is a way you punish yourself? Does the punishment fit the crime? It probably doesn't.
6. Torturing yourself with guilt doesn't make you a better person. Learning does. So what can you learn from your past experiences with guilt?
7. Whose standards are you failing to live up to?

GOING DEEPER

"I, even I, am he who blots out
your transgressions, for my own sake,
and remembers your sins no more."

(Isa. 43:25 niv)

Fixing our eyes on Jesus, the pioneer and perfecter of faith. For the joy set before him he endured the cross, scorning its shame, and sat down at the right hand of the throne of God.

(Heb. 12:2 niv)

Let us draw near to God with a sincere heart and with the full assurance that faith brings, having our hearts sprinkled to cleanse us from a guilty conscience and having our bodies washed with pure water.

(Heb. 10:22 niv)

They must be committed to the mystery of the faith now revealed and must live with a clear conscience.

(1 Tim. 3:9)

Chapter 12: Prayerlessness

1. Is prayer difficult for you? If so, what about it makes it so difficult?
2. What is your greatest obstacle to consistent prayer right now?
3. What are some of the consequences you have faced because of a lack of prayer?
4. How is prayer the surest remedy to any bad habit you might have?
5. How is prayerlessness evidence that you are backsliding?
6. Can a person who doesn't pray honor God?
7. To what extent is our prayerlessness due to not seeing our great needs? How can we be more aware of our true needs?

GOING DEEPER

And the Holy Spirit helps us in our weakness. For example, we don't know what God wants us to pray for. But the Holy Spirit prays for us with groanings that cannot be expressed in words. And the Father who knows all hearts knows what the Spirit is saying, for the Spirit pleads for us believers in harmony with God's own will.

(Rom. 8:26–27)

I tell you the truth, anyone who believes in me will do the same works I have done, and even greater works, because I am going to be with the Father. You can ask for anything in my name, and I will do it, so that the Son can bring glory to the Father. Yes, ask me for anything in my name, and I will do it!

(John 14:12–14)

I urge you, first of all, to pray for all people. Ask God to help them; intercede on their behalf, and give thanks for them.

(1 Tim. 2:1)

One day Jesus told his disciples a story to show that they should always pray and never give up.

(Luke 18:1)

ACKNOWLEDGMENTS

For many years I've felt like God was prompting me to write. And on several occasions, I would begin a book, but the hectic schedule of pastoring a large church always seemed to get in the way of my commitment to complete it. But after I had finished preaching a series of messages on getting rid of bad habits, Stephen Arterburn approached me and said, "What are you waiting for? This series is your book!" Steve, you have continued to be such an encouragement and inspiration in my life. Thank you for that. And the incredible foreword you wrote for this book is so appreciated.

Writing a book is different than writing a sermon. For thirty-five years I've been writing sermons, but I didn't know the first thing about writing a book. Mark Atteberry, thank you for coaching me and encouraging me along the way of this project and for always being available to answer questions.

John Dickerson and Randy Frazee are both such great authors, pastors, and friends. Thank you for constantly encouraging me along this process.

This book is also the product of an incredible team of editors and staff at Thomas Nelson. Thank you, Lauren, Jenny, Kristen, and so many others who were always quick to encourage and help me through this process.

I am so grateful to my agent, Greg Johnson, for taking me as a client and encouraging me on each new step I needed to take. I am also grateful for the encouragement from all the people who wrote words of endorsement for this book.

The staff at Northview Church are amazing. They were with me through the entire process, always asking for updates on how the book was coming along. I'm humbled that God has sent me such a remarkable team of people to work alongside.

And to my family, thank you, for your love and encouragement. To my mother, Joyce, thank you for loving and encouraging me and for always praying for me.

To my son, Ryan, and daughter, Jenni, you are both better writers and smarter than I will ever be. I am so proud of who you have become and appreciate your encouragement more than you can know. And to my son-in-law, Andy, and my daughter-in-law, Shannon, I appreciate your encouragement as well. Thank you, Andy, for setting up my website.

To my wife, Sandy, this project would have never been completed without your help. You have read every chapter, you have given me constructive ideas on things that would improve the book, and when I needed to write you sacrificed our personal time together so I could complete the book. I can't imagine what my life would be without you!

To seven of my favorite people in the world, my grandkids—Jake, Lauren, Jillian, Emily, Claira, Desi, and Griffin—you guys bring so much joy into my life. I love you!

And finally, to my readers, thank you for picking up a copy of this book and allowing me to share a part of my life with you! I hope it has inspired you to be all that God wants you to be.

NOTES

CHAPTER 1: PRIDE

1. Doug Wead, *All the President's Children: Triumph and Tragedy in the Lives of America's First Families* (New York: Atria Books, 2003), 107–8.
2. C. S. Lewis, *Mere Christianity* (New York: HarperOne, 2001), 122.
3. Lewis, *Mere Christianity*, 128.

CHAPTER 2: ANGER

1. FBI: UCR, "Expanded Homicide Data Table 10: Murder Circumstances by Relationship, 2018," Federal Bureau of Investigation, https://ucr.fbi.gov/crime-in-the-u.s/2018/crime-in-the-u.s.-2018/tables/expanded-homicide-data-table-10.xls.
2. "Child Maltreatment Statistics in the U.S.," American SPCC, https://americanspcc.org/child-abuse-statistics/.
3. Alexandra Sifferlin, "Is This Teen Angst or an Uncontrollable Anger Disorder?," *TIME*, July 3, 2012, https://healthland.time.com/2012/07/03/is-this-teen-angst-or-an-uncontrollable-anger-disorder/.
4. Allan N. Schwartz, "Exercise, Can It Reduce Angry Feelings?," MentalHelp.net, https://www.mentalhelp.net/exercise/and-anger/.
5. Anne Lamott, *Traveling Mercies: Some Thoughts on Faith* (New York: Anchor, 1999), 134.
6. Lewis B. Smedes, *The Art of Forgiving* (New York: Ballantine Books, 1996), 178.

CHAPTER 3: EXCUSES

1. Calvin Miller, "Self-Importance: The Helpless, Hopeless Man: A Covenant with Your Self-Importance," Preaching.com (sermon), https://www.preaching.com/sermons/self-importance-the-helpless-hopeless-man-a-covenant-with-your-self-importance/.
2. Jim Rohn, Goodreads, https://www.goodreads.com/quotes/297774-if-you-really-want-to-do-something-you-ll-find-a.
3. "15 Motivational Quotes to Stop Making Excuses," Success.com, March 23, 2017, https://www.success.com/15-motivational-quotes-to-stop-making-excuses/.
4. Laura Schlessinger, Quotes, https://www.quotes.net/quote/17344.
5. Gabriel Meurier, Know Your Quotes, http://www.knowyourquotes.com/He-Who-Excuses-Himself-Accuses-Himself-Gabriel-Meurier.html.
6. Marc Santora, "Teenagers' Suit Says McDonald's Made Them Obese," *New York Times*, November 21, 2002, https://www.nytimes.com/2002/11/21/nyregion/teenagers-suit-says-mcdonald-s-made-them-obese.html.

CHAPTER 4: LUST

1. Charles R. Swindoll, *Come Before Winter and Share My Hope* (Portland, OR: Multnomah Press, 1994), 32; quoted in "Closing the Door to Lust, Part One," Insight for Living, June 12, 2017, https://insight.org/resources/daily-devotional/individual/closing-the-door-to-lust-part-one.
2. "Generation Rx.com: How Young People Use the Internet for Health Information," The Henry J. Kaiser Family Foundation, December 2001, https://www.kff.org/wp-content/uploads/2001/11/3202-genrx-report.pdf, 12.
3. Covenant Eyes, *Porn Stats: 250+ Facts, Quotes, and Statistics About Pornography Use (2015 Edition)* (Owosso, MI: Covenant Eyes, 2015), https://www.bevillandassociates.com/wp-content/uploads/2015/05/2015-porn-stats-covenant-eyes-1.pdf, 14.
4. US Department of Justice, "Post Hearing Memorandum of Points

and Authorities," *ACLU v. Reno*, 929 F. Supp. 824, 1996; quoted in Covenant Eyes, *Porn Stats*, 13.

5. Mark Regnerus, David Gordon, and Joseph Price, "Documenting Pornography Use in America: A Comparative Analysis of Methodological Approaches," *Journal of Sex Research*, December 18, 2015, https://www.tandfonline.com/doi/full/10.1080/00224499.2015.1096886.
6. Jacquelyn Ekern, "Sexual Addiction Causes, Statistics, Addiction Signs, Symptoms & Side Effects," Addiction Hope, April 29, 2019, https://www.addictionhope.com/sexual-addiction/.
7. Luscombe, "Porn and the Threat to Virility," *TIME*, March 31, 2016, https://time.com/magazine/us/4277492/april-11th-2016-vol-187-no-13-u-s/.
8. Luscombe, "Porn and the Threat to Virility."
9. Lee Strobel, *God's Outrageous Claims* (Grand Rapids: Zondervan, 2005), 173.
10. Jane E. Brody, "Cybersex Gives Birth to a Psychological Disorder," *New York Times*, May 16, 2000, https://archive.nytimes.com/www.nytimes.com/library/national/science/health/051600hth-behavior-cybersex.html.
11. Rory Reid and Dan Gray, *Confronting Your Spouse's Pornography Problem* (Sandy, UT: Silverleaf Press, 2006), 17.

CHAPTER 5: CYNICISM

1. Your Dictionary, s.v. "cynicism," https://www.yourdictionary.com/cynicism.
2. Paul Miller, *A Praying Life: Connecting with God in a Distracting World* (Colorado Springs: NavPress, 2009), 64, 68.
3. Carey Nieuwhof, *Didn't See It Coming: Overcoming the 7 Greatest Challenges That No One Expects and Everyone Experiences* (Colorado Springs: Waterbrook, 2018), 25.

CHAPTER 6: WORRY

1. *Merriam-Webster*, s.v. "worry," https://www.merriam-webster.com/dictionary/worry.

2. This quote has been attributed to multiple people.
3. Erma Bombeck, Goodreads, https://www.goodreads.com/quotes/140315-worry-is-like-a-rocking-chair-it-gives-you-something.
4. Earl Nightingale, "The Fog of Worry (Only 8% of Worries Are Worth It)," Nightingale Conant, https://www.nightingale.com/articles/the-fog-of-worry-only-8-of-worries-are-worth-it/.
5. "How Worry Affects Your Body," WebMD, August 18, 2019, https://www.webmd.com/anxiety-panic/ss/slideshow-worry-body-effects.
6. "Charles Mayo," Today in Science History, https://todayinsci.com/M/Mayo_Charles/MayoCharles-Quotations.htm.
7. Glen E. Clifton, *Being "In Christ": We Have Victory!* (Bloomington, IN: WestBow Press, 2012), 173.
8. Jean M. Twenge, "Studies Show Normal Children Today Report More Anxiety Than Child Psychiatric Patients in the 1950s," American Psychological Association, December 2000, https://www.apa.org/news/press/releases/2000/12/anxiety.
9. Robert A. Jonas, ed., *The Essential Henri Nouwen* (Boston; Shambhala, 2009), 132.
10. Max Lucado, *Life to the Full* (Nashville: Thomas Nelson, 2012), 50.

CHAPTER 7: COMPLAINING

1. Guy Winch, "How to Deal with Chronic Complainers," *Psychology Today*, July 15, 2011, https://www.psychologytoday.com/us/blog/the-squeaky-wheel/201107/how-deal-chronic-complainers.
2. "Paul Molitor Quote," AZ Quotes, https://www.azquotes.com/quote/1023952.
3. A. W. Tozer, *The Next Chapter After the Last* (Chicago: Moody Bible Institute, 1987), 16.
4. Eckhart Tolle, *The Power of Now* (Vancouver, BC: Namaste Publishing, 1999), 82.
5. "Man Robs Wendy's; Calls Back Twice to Complain About Loot," KHQ News, August 5, 2010, https://www.khq.com/news/man-robs-wendys-calls-back-twice-to-complain-about-loot/article_eccbb3a7-a7e5-5ece-bd1a-0a534a9fdfb7.html.

6. Mike Martinez, "Mike's the Stupid News: Bank Robber Arrested After He Returns to Complain," KISS FM El Paso, October 25, 2012, https://kisselpaso.com/mikes-the-stupid-news-bank-robber-arrested-after-he-returns-to-complain/.
7. Will Bowen, "Stop Complaining, Start Living," Will Bowen (website), https://www.willbowen.com/complaintfree/.
8. "Wesley Responds to Criticism," Sermon Central, April 19, 2011, https://www.sermoncentral.com/sermon-illustrations/78779/wesley-responds-to-criticism-by-sermoncentral.
9. Laura Marham, "The Average Person Complains 30 Times a Day . . . Would You Like to Stop?," *Active Family*, https://www.activefamilymag.com/average-person-complains-30-times-day-like-stop.
10. Alice-Azania Jarvis, "Here's What Happens When You Actually Quit Complaining for 21 Days," *Woman's Day*, March 8, 2016, https://www.womansday.com/life/inspirational-stories/a54051/stop-complaining-21-days/.
11. Jarvis, "Quit Complaining."
12. Michael Zigarelli, "Gratitude: Pathway to Permanent Change," Christianity 9 to 5, http://www.christianity9to5.org/gratitude-pathway-to-permanent-change/.
13. Zigarelli, "Gratitude."

CHAPTER 8: WORKAHOLISM

1. Livia Areas-Holmblad, "The Similarity Between Workaholism and Alcoholism," Addiction Now, March 19, 2017, https://www.drugaddictionnow.com/2017/03/19/the-similarity-between-workaholism-and-alcoholism/.
2. Areas-Holmblad, "Similarity Between Workaholism and Alcoholism."
3. Lieke ten Brummelhuis and Nancy P. Rothbard, "How Being a Workaholic Differs from Working Long Hours—and Why That Matters for Your Health," *Harvard Business Review*, March 22, 2018, https://hbr.org/2018/03/how-being-a-workaholic-differs-from-working-long-hours-and-why-that-matters-for-your-health.

4. Mara Tyler, "Work Addiction," Healthline, updated December 19, 2017, https://www.healthline.com/health/addiction/work.
5. "The 12 Steps of Workaholics Anonymous," American Addiction Centers, https://www.recovery.org/support-groups/workaholics-anonymous/.

CHAPTER 9: LYING

1. Pamela Meyer, "How to Spot a Liar," TEDGlobal 2011, July 2011, https://www.ted.com/talks/pamela_meyer_how_to_spot_a_liar.
2. Lisa Firestone, "Why We Lie and How to Stop," *Psychology Today*, September 23, 2013, https://www.psychologytoday.com/us/blog/compassion-matters/201309/why-we-lie-and-how-stop.
3. Bernice Kanner, "Americans Lie, or So They Say," *New York Times*, June 2, 1996, https://www.nytimes.com/1996/06/02/archives/americans-lie-or-so-they-say.html.
4. Twain Quotes, http://www.twainquotes.com/Truth.html.
5. "Reports of Mark Twain's quip about his death are greatly misquoted," ThisDayinQuotes.com, June 2, 2018, http://www.thisdayinquotes.com/2010/06/reports-of-my-death-are-greatly.html.
6. Opie Read, *Mark Twain and I* (Chicago: Reilly & Lee, 1940), 34.

CHAPTER 10: IDOLATRY

1. "Billy Graham's Daughter: Anne Graham Lotz Regarding the Events of 9/11," The Prayer Foundation, September 13, 2001, https://www.prayerfoundation.org/billy_grahams_daughter.htm.
2. Winston Churchill, QuoteFancy, https://quotefancy.com/quote/940080/Winston-Churchill-Never-let-a-good-crisis-go-to-waste.
3. Timothy Keller, *Counterfeit Gods* (New York: Penguin Books, 2009), xix.
4. Kyle Idleman, *Gods at War: Defeating the Idols That Battle for Your Heart* (Grand Rapids: Zondervan, 2013), 27.
5. Jory MacKay, "Screen Time Stats 2019: Here's How Much You Use Your Phone During the Workday," RescueTime (blog), March 21, 2019, https://blog.rescuetime.com/screen-time-stats-2018/.
6. Rebecca Joy Stanborough, "How to Tell If You Could Be

Addicted to Your Phone," Healthline, October 17, 2019, https://www.healthline.com/health/mental-health/cell-phone-addiction.

7. C. S. Lewis, *Mere Christianity* (1952; repr., San Francisco: HarperSanFrancisco, 2001), 135–36.

CHAPTER 11: GUILT

1. Francis J. Flynn, "Defend Your Research: Guilt-Ridden People Make Great Leaders," *Harvard Business Review* January–February 2011, https://hbr.org/2011/01/defend-your-research-guilt-ridden-people-make-great-leaders/ar/1.
2. Paul Coughlin, "Healthy Guilt vs. False and Harmful Guilt," Focus on the Family, February 1, 2008, https://www.focusonthefamily.com/get-help/healthy-guilt-vs-false-and-harmful-guilt/.
3. Jessica Van Roekel, "10 Ways to Overcome Your 'If-Only' Regrets," iBelieve.com, https://www.ibelieve.com/faith/10-ways-to-overcome-your-if-only-regrets.html.
4. Chris Weller, "There's a Place for Thieves with a Guilty Conscience to Return Money to the Government Anonymously," *Business Insider*, March 12, 2017, https://www.businessinsider.com/conscience-fund-us-treasury-2017-3.
5. Charles Stanley, *The Gift of Forgiveness* (Nashville: Thomas Nelson, 1991), 116.
6. Haddon W. Robinson, "1929 Rose Bowl," Bible.org, February 2, 2009, https://bible.org/illustration/1929-rose-bowl.
7. Coughlin, "Healthy Guilt."

CHAPTER 12: PRAYERLESSNESS

1. Marvin Knight, "The Cause of Prayerlessness," Church at South Mountain, http://casm.org/the-cause-of-prayerlessness/.
2. John Bunyan, Goodreads, https://www.goodreads.com/quotes/401457-prayer-will-make-a-man-cease-from-sin-or-sin.
3. "10 Quotes from Billy Graham on Prayer," Billy Graham Library, March 5, 2019, https://billygrahamlibrary.org/blog-10-quotes-from-billy-graham-on-prayer/.
4. "10 Quotes from Billy Graham," Billy Graham Library.

EPILOGUE

1. R. L. Hymers Jr., "Breaking the Chains of Destructive Habits," Sermons for the World, November 11, 2001, https://www.rlhymersjr.com/Online_Sermons/11-11-01AM_BreakingTheChainsOfDestructiveHabits.html.
2. "Habits," Biblia.Work, https://www.biblia.work/sermons/habits-2/.
3. Mark Twain, Goodreads, https://www.goodreads.com/quotes/219455-the-secret-of-getting-ahead-is-getting-started-the-secret.

ABOUT THE AUTHOR

Steve Poe, lead pastor of Northview Church in central Indiana, got his start in ministry at Caring First Church in St. Joseph, Missouri, where he pastored for thirteen years. After transitioning to Northview Church in 1999, Steve has led with a passion to reach the unchurched.

Steve started his career in the business world, first opening three restaurants and franchising two others. He was also part owner and operator of a radio station, which soon became a Christian radio station. His third business investment was to open a financial planning firm as well as a commodity trading group. Although he loved the business world, he sensed God calling him into full-time ministry.

Steve's background in business gives him a distinctive understanding and heart for professionals. Under his leadership, Northview Church has grown from one campus in Carmel, Indiana, to thirteen campuses throughout central Indiana. In 2018 Steve received an honorary doctorate from Taylor University.

Known to his friends and colleagues as a leader, teacher, and visionary, Steve has served for more than twenty years as lead pastor of Northview Church. Under his leadership, the church has grown from five hundred to more than twelve thousand in attendance.

Steve has spoken at major events such as the North American Christian Convention, Truth at Work Leadership Conference, Next Level 2020, Building God's Way church growth conference, and chapel for Taylor University.

Steve and his wife, Sandy, whom he refers to as his best friend, enjoy traveling together and going to movies. They love to spend time with their two children and their spouses, Ryan (Shannon) and Jenni (Andy), and their seven grandchildren, Jake, Emily, Desi, Lauren, Jillian, Claira, and Griffin.